Race and Sexuality

Race and Sexuality

Salvador Vidal-Ortiz,
Brandon Andrew Robinson
and Cristina Khan

polity

First published in 2018 by Polity Press

Polity Press
65 Bridge Street
Cambridge CB2 1UR, UK

Polity Press
101 Station Landing
Suite 300
Medford, MA 02155, USA

ISBN-13: 978-1-5095-1383-3
ISBN-13: 978-1-5095-1384-0(pb)

A catalogue record for this book is available from the British Library.

Library of Congress Cataloging-in-Publication Data

Names: Vidal-Ortiz, Salvador, author. | Robinson, Brandon Andrew, author. |
  Khan, Cristina, author.
Title: Race and sexuality / Salvador Vidal-Ortiz, Brandon Andrew Robinson,
  Cristina Khan.
Description: Cambridge, UK ; Medford, MA : Polity Press, 2018. |
  Includes bibliographical references and index.
Identifiers: LCCN 2017036534 (print) | LCCN 2017046358 (ebook) |
  ISBN 9781509513871 (Epub) | ISBN 9781509513833 (hardback) |
  ISBN 9781509513840 (pbk.)
Subjects: LCSH: Race. | Sex. | Sexual orientation. | Discrimination.
Classification: LCC HT1523 (ebook) | LCC HT1523 .V53 2018 (print) |
  DDC 305–dc23
LC record available at https://lccn.loc.gov/2017036534

Typeset in 11 on 13 pt Sabon by Toppan Best-set Premedia Limited
Printed and bound in Great Britain by Clays Ltd, St. Ives PLC

Contents

Acknowledgments

Working together in a shared authorship project is always a labor of love. For many, this labor is only sometimes a joy; more often than not, this collaborative labor is a source of irritation or tension. When co-authoring is more a blessing than a curse, whether you are the faculty member, the post-doctoral fellow, or the doctoral candidate, you know you've won the lottery. We are lucky enough to have found each other, trusted each other, and endured the work (and solace, and rejoinder) of this project. In the end, the labor and the responsibility fall on the three of us but, truth be told, there isn't much we would do differently. The many Skype sessions and brainstorming moments made the heart of this project beat, giving life to the words and ideas in this book.

We all wish to thank Jonathan Skerrett for believing in this book project. To the various members of the Polity team who supported this venture – from bringing our ideas to fruition with a wonderful cover to the reviewers of the text who offered their insight and guidance – thank you. Polity was ever-accommodating and supportive throughout this venture; for this we could not be more grateful!

Introduction

The connections between race and sexuality[1] are constant in our lives, yet we do not always have a developed sense of how processes of race (from racial identification to racial hierarchies) are linked to sexuality (such as sexual behavior, desire, identity, or other aspects of sexuality). However, stereotypes assumed to be linked to racial minorities and/or sexual and erotic communities abound in the media and in the news, in everyday interactions, and lurk in our imaginary of individuals, members of minoritized groups of peoples (be it by race and/or sexuality), and even based on nationality or the labeling of a whole ethno-racial group as having particular traits. Recent mainstream media events that demonstrate the power of racial stereotypes include moments such as the 2014 Emmys, where Sofia Vergara was rotated on a pedestal to showcase her curvy body while the chairman of the Academy of Television Arts and Sciences proclaimed that their show is "always giving the viewer something compelling to watch" (Vidal-Ortiz 2016). More recently, comedian Steve Harvey stated in January 2017 that the book *How to Date a White Woman: A Practical Guide for Asian Men* by Adam Quan only needed to be a page long because white women would never find Asian men desirable. Just as stereotypes rooted in race and sexuality are plentiful in the media, those relative to sexuality label gay men and bisexual people as promiscuous, and those relative to race label black people and Latinas/os as hypersexual, working to establish white heterosexuality as the norm.[2] These ideas and images shape the material realities experienced by individuals on all sides of the production and consumption of such stereotypes.

Whether you are reading this book in the United States, in the United Kingdom, or somewhere else, the ways in which we "connect the dots" about people, events, and life experiences really depends on how we think about, and the exposure we have to, processes that connect race and sexuality. Consider your local news and how international, transnational, and global processes are presented: whether reporters are discussing a range of issues faced by countries being invaded through militarization and the subsequent displacement of hundreds of thousands of people, or drawing attention to certain ethno-racial minority groups who quickly get connected to sex work and trafficking, or the political processes of regulating a nation's border against the flow of immigrants, or the fight for democracy in some other country or region that often gets connected to lesbian, gay, bisexual, and transgender (LGBT) rights (or a fight against the veiled woman) as markers of underdevelopment – all of those illustrations enforce a reading of hierarchies between nations (and their people) that bring up race (and migration) and/or sexuality (and gender oppression) as markers of progress (or backwardness).[3] We are provided – as audiences – with multiple messages that either signify a connection between race and sexuality (as in the case of criminality, or poverty, or hypersexuality, or stereotypes around reproduction) or that attempt to disentangle (or, at least, try to make invisible) their inherent relationship altogether (think about government or parliament as places that are often racially homogeneous and normatively heterosexual).

Our focus in *Race and Sexuality* is to bring forth the unique power dynamics embedded in the relationship between systems that are mutually constitutive of each other in social analyses. Our pedagogical goal is to show how social difference is foundational to social life and how these dimensions – race and sexuality – interface. Figures such as the "welfare queen"[4] (Bensonsmith 2005; see also Cohen 1997; Ferguson 2004), the transgender woman of color (Vidal-Ortiz 2009; see also Spade 2015 [2011]), and men on the "down low" (Robinson and Vidal-Ortiz 2013; Vidal-Ortiz and Robinson 2016) are racialized and sexualized constructs that fuel stereotypes about certain groups of people in ways that do not affect all members of society in the same way. These imaginaries are often utilized to launch neoliberal political agendas that continue class divisions, subsequently affecting individuals in different social locations quite incongruously.[5] While we are all impacted, we are also all implicated in the dynamics of domination and subordination, which are sustained through the ongoing production of race and sexuality biases operating in tandem with (and in and through) each other, and which further individual notions of people's marginalization.

While everyone – *as an individual* – experiences being racialized and sexualized (and thus white, heterosexual people experience this process too), those readings are filled with distinct structural meanings that impact the material and lived experiences of people based on how their social locations and demographics are socially understood. As we discuss in chapter 4, a black (or Latina) woman may be seen as dependent on the state (for food stamps, or for changing their migration status, if undocumented), yet a white woman's raced and sexual representation is often more wide-ranged and, while often based on perceptions of innocence, white women's representations are particularly scripted along a continuum unavailable to other women. The amplitude or reduced number of options in these representations tend to be profitable specifically, but not exclusively, in terms of erotic labor and sexualized imaginaries.

In *Race and Sexuality*, we illustrate and unpack the intricate relationship (seldom explored together) between, on the one hand, race and class readings and, on the other, gender and sexuality. Because we see these overarching elements as operating in tandem with one another, discursively and in everyday lived experiences, this book proposes a more nuanced way to understand this relationship through analytical discussions, popular culture examples, and summaries of specific case studies that showcase our contribution. We do so to more actively produce an analysis that does not foreground traditional understandings of race as more important than sexuality, or sexuality as a more central analytic category than race – those singular analyses produce, in the end, dull efforts at critical thinking. We pay attention to disciplinary contributions to the study of race and sexuality in the introduction; we save the discussion about topics/ areas of study within the disciplines, as well as interdisciplinary ones, for chapter 1.

What follows in this introduction is a section with definitions of terms and concepts central to our book, with the goal of providing a common ground for our readership. This layout is followed by the sociohistorical context through which we situate the book. We close the introduction by centering the disciplines that have grappled with ideas around race and sexuality to elucidate their unevenness and success in tackling these categories' co-constitutive relationship. We end by providing an overview of what is to come in the book, and the political stakes in taking seriously the concept of *racialized sexualities*. Our goal is to leave the reader with a strong sense of how race and sexuality are always mutually constituted (at times visibly connected and at times with one aspect foregrounded and the other implicit), and that to see race and sexuality as discrete analytical categories fails to capture their intertwined and complex relationship.

Central terms and concepts

In this section, we discuss the terms we often use in the book in order to have a shared understanding of the basic tenets of our arguments. Like other social scientists, we understand race as a cultural and social construct, but, in doing so, we do not adhere to the popular notion that one can simply deconstruct race (because, as students and others often say wrongfully, since something is a social construction, it can be undone). It takes generational efforts and decades to map out a different racial terrain, given the linkages that exist between race, privilege, and access to resources. Thus this undoing of race is not an individually achievable project.

When we speak of race and ethnicity, we subscribe to an understanding that whatever boundaries between the ethnic and the racial are in any given territory (say, the United States), they speak to common groups of people that belong to larger umbrella terms (such as Asian, Pacific Islander, Native American, and Latin American or US Latina/o, which encompass several, sometimes dozens of, different nationally based groups – what is often called pan-ethnic), as well as people grouped along the lines of readings of the body as inherently different groups (such as black or white people) that are read, interpreted, and phenotypically classified as belonging to one category (for example, Asian), and not another (for instance, black). Although mixed-race/multiracial people may be seen as challenging these categories at times (and are sometimes portrayed as a sign of a "post-racial" society), multiracial people often get placed in one of the already established racial categories within (any given) society. For those multiracial people who may have certain types of light-skin privilege or white heritage, they may become "honorary whites," maintaining the hierarchical racial system that subjugates black people and bodies (Bonilla-Silva 2013). Mixed-race/multiracial people appear to occupy a contradictory space, whereby they may both be seen as challenging the racial binary in society and also may be interpreted to uphold the binary and its hierarchies.

We often refer to or use a shorter term that we prefer, "ethno-racial," to convey the relationship between race and ethnicity throughout the book. Ethno-racial alludes to a previously significant construct – that of ethnic identity and ethnic communities – from earlier multicultural or pluralist analyses (e.g., "the melting pot"), yet conjures more recent analyses of "ethnic" that defy that previous lens and that do not subscribe to previously dominant paradigms often linked to immigration (e.g., assimilationist approaches). Thus this "ethnic" is combined with a racial construct to converge government-defined institutional categories like the US Census with popular notions of the ethnic and the racial as cohabiting. We do this convergence of ethnic and racial because, while distinctions have been made between one's being ethnicized versus being racialized (Urciuoli 1996; see our discussion in chapter 2), both of these processes capture inherent racial readings (albeit with various cultural and social readings of "difference" or "danger"). A word of caution: we do not use "ethnic" in the more traditional European use of heritage; as well, we stay away from the common US usage that presumes ethnic as cultural elements that code national heritage attributes (as in Italian, Italian-American, little Italy, and/or foods and customs assumed to be representative of such nationality-based heritage groups). We also do not refer to ethnic to assume innate characteristics of racial or pan-ethnic groups (such as "all Latinas are voluptuous or hypersexual," or "white men can't dance").

Race, and being raced, is established in clear demarcations of understandings of difference in and through a hierarchical reading of groups supposedly agreed upon (explicitly or, more to the current times, implicitly) as superior or inferior. Race and racial readings vary according to the racial formation processes in any given geopolitical context – the term "racial formation" references the sociohistorical formations of solidifying race and racial groups into distinctive, oppositional categories (Omi and Winant 1986). (As processes, they take multiple decades to enact, if not longer – these are not moments, or temporalities, in racial systems, but shifts that become rooted through both structural arrangements and the participation of people in any given territory.) Racial readings act as commonly shared understandings – not only of the value of a given racial group but of the permeability or movement into and outside that construct. To put it another way, in certain spaces it seems desirable to become white, with group boundaries threatened by sought-after changes in skin tone (for instance, with the cosmetic advances to "lighten" one's skin) and, in others, whiteness is actually measured in relation to economic resources, often making symbolic racial mobility possible (Bonilla-Silva 2013). However, all members of a given geopolitical territory must be in some kind of agreement, otherwise the racial movement (or passing through certain categories) cannot be accomplished.

"Racialization" refers to the markings of people previously unmarked (Omi and Winant 1986). Omi and Winant later defined racialization as "the extension of racial meaning to a previously racially unclassified relationship, social practice, or group" (2015: 13), wherein racialization becomes the anchor for the discussion of racial readings and understandings of race. Racialization is a sociohistorical concept developed to better explain US racial formation, which was based on the colonization and exploitation of the land, human power, and distribution of the goods based on such exploitation. Social relations, cemented on the creation of terms such as white and black, structured the nation-state through slavery and then through the Civil War (roughly the late part of the seventeenth century and into the nineteenth century). Individuals who came from various countries or regions that we have come to identify as black or white were consolidated into such groups through a very specific political, economic, and social process of a raced and classed order. This racialization sustained such a powerful binary of whiteness and blackness (while eclipsing the existence of Native Americans) that it still serves as our social, cultural, and racial compass today, further proving the power of that racial formation system. But the racial formation so central to the USAmerican[6] psyche, structured on racial binaries, was also structuring other elements such as gender, sexuality, and class (Holland 2012; see also Ferguson 2004), making it more complex then and today (see Martinez HoSang, LaBennett, and Pulido 2012).

Similarly, to speak of sexuality is to invoke a set of specific social arrangements. Sexuality is also socially constructed, whereby sexual meanings, identities, and categories are socially situated within a given historical point in time and negotiated intersubjectively (Foucault 1978 [1976]; Epstein 1994). To fully conceptualize our understandings of sexuality, we find it imperative to define the following terms: sexual orientation, gender identity, and the gendering of sexuality. Sexual orientation refers to how we define a person's sexual identity relative to their own gender and whom they are attracted to. Iterations of sexual orientation include heterosexual, bisexual, gay or lesbian, pan-sexual, or other types of orientation. However, attraction, sexual behavior, or the erotic in a person's life may "spill over" these sexual orientation categories; that is, attraction, behavior, and other forms of eroticism are not in neat alignment, or always easily contained, within the categories, even in seemingly fluid terms such as bisexual or pan-sexual.

Gender identity indexes how individuals understand their gender and does not necessarily correspond to one's gender assigned at birth. Gender, gender identity, and gender expression are also complex in their relationship to each other, as well as to notions of sex; furthermore, gendering takes shape in racialized ways (Kitch 2009) and in reference to corporeality, embodiment, and body shape, but also class, citizenship, and culture. The gendering of sexuality speaks to the conflation of gender and sexuality, and asserts that one's gender is informed by one's self-concepts and others' perception of one's sexuality, such that to be a man is imagined also to be heterosexual.

Sex, gender, and sexuality are intrinsically connected – and they organize the set of values around expectations of being sexed, gendered, and one's sexuality. These values are not "natural" but part of our social organization. One main undertaking in unmasking the social meaning of sexual identities and relations is Adrienne Rich's (1980) concept of "compulsory heterosexuality." This concept is often credited as a foundational idea within queer theory for it describes heterosexuality, in western societies, as a patriarchal institution that tries to make obligatory heterosexual relations, constructing non-heterosexual relations, such as lesbian relations, as abnormal. Furthermore, Gayle Rubin, in her influential 1984 essay titled "Thinking Sex," introduced the idea of the "charmed circle." Despite the conviction that one's sexuality is a personal and intimate detail of one's life, Rubin's work uncovered the relationship between sexuality and the state. According to Rubin, sexuality becomes politically mapped and valued along binary lines of "good" or "bad" in concentric circles. In most western societies, sex is often seen as dangerous and constructed within a negativity discourse (Rubin 1993 [1984]). However, certain sexuality – primarily marital, reproductive heterosexuality – is hierarchically ranked as the most socially respectable, conferring upon individuals who enact and embody this form of sexuality many rewards, including legal, social, physical, material, and institutional benefits. This ranking creates a sexual stigma against those who do not perform this mode of sexual enactment and embodiment, relegating non-heterosexual individuals and non-heteronormative sexual practices to a lower realm of social approvability. This logic shapes many state practices and policies, not limited to access to marriage and state-sanctioned benefits for monogamous, heterosexual, married couples. (In Rubin's analysis, what's not evident – race and racializing practices – emerges as an important silence; we denote how race becomes an inherent addition to the aforementioned socially disapproved beings and stigmatized categories.)

Sexuality is also mapped along a hetero/homo binary that shapes people's thinking of sexuality and that can limit people's sexual enactments, embodiments, and desires (Sedgwick 1990). This binary is so powerful that men who engage in any form of same-sex sexual behavior are often seen as gay, erasing the possibility of bisexuality or any other identity. Likewise, bisexuality is seen as illegitimate within the hetero/homo binary, whereby bisexuality is constructed as a "phase" one goes through to then become one's "authentic" sexual self (Callis 2013). In this regard, the hetero/homo binary structures much of life and is linked to the gender binary of man/woman, their reproductive capacities, and the expectation of romantic, dyad relationships, whether in same- or opposite-sex unions.

Therefore, the meaning of sexuality is also tied to gender, whereby in many societies gender is often seen as a binary of man and woman. Within this binary, men and women are seen as "naturally" different and as having complementary characteristics. This binary framing erases the lives of people who do not fit neatly into it, including some transgender people, genderqueer people, and gender-expansive and non-binary individuals. Indeed, the term "cisgender" has been coined to acknowledge the privileges that people who identify with and conform to the gender they were assigned at birth receive in society compared to transgender and gender-expansive individuals.

Today, sexuality and gender are often intimately related within societies. Sexual desire – one's erotic longings and fantasies or how one thinks about one's sex life (Laumann et al. 1994) – is often related to one's gender desires (i.e., a desire for a man and/or a woman and/or a person with another gender identity/presentation). These desires and attractions often play a main role in the construction of one's sexual identity. If a woman is attracted exclusively or mainly to men, she may identify as heterosexual. Likewise, to be a man is often to be perceived/assumed to be heterosexual, that is, dominant notions of masculinity rely upon dominant notions of (hetero)sexuality. However, this is based on a construction of a gender binary and a cisgender identity; transgender people tend to challenge the assumption that to have a sexual orientation, one must identify with or require a gender (Vidal-Ortiz 2002). But not all transgender people reject a gender identification of themselves and their partners; furthermore, a fluid set of identities for some transgender people may not always represent the same experience for their partners, especially when coming from gay, lesbian, or bisexual communities (Pfeffer 2014).

Sociohistorical context that organizes our book's argument

Although a lot of the examples provided in this book are contemporary, it is important to establish the racial/sexual specificity in US soil in a sociohistorical context. To speak of racial formations as the foundation of the United States (Omi and Winant 1986) requires a brief discussion of the raced and classed aspects of slavery and the wealthy, and the classed, raced, and gender lines sustained in the seventeenth and eighteenth centuries. Such racial formation – already classed and demarcating a distinctive set of social relations between the two established genders – was compulsorily heterosexual as well. Furthermore, while sexuality was not as visible in these social relations among people, racial/sexual lines were not to be crossed: white women's sexuality was innocent and protected, while African enslaved women's sense of self was not acknowledged, much less respected, by the masters, who often saw African women's sexuality as just (re-)producing more slaves. After slavery ended, African-American males could not demonstrate attraction toward white women, thus racially restricting a sexual crossing. Late in the 1880s and into the 1890s, in the so-called post-Reconstruction Era, the increased public portrayal of black men as rapists, combined with the previously mentioned gendered-racialized perception of white women as innocent, resulted in the lynchings of African-American men (Bederman 1995; Gunning 1996; see also Kitch 2009). The abolition of slavery only symbolically broke some aspects of this divide, but it would not succeed in formulating a racial/sexual crossing that permitted cross-racial relationships for at least another century.

In addition to constructing a lasting stigma against cross-racial relationships, black sexual politics in a US context was ultimately shaped by and through the binary juxtaposition of presumed white (moral) sexuality against black (immoral) hypersexuality, which was almost always constructed as criminal (it was certainly seen as deviant enough to be suspect). Collins (2004) links norms of sexuality to raced and classed epithets born from this era (e.g., the jezebel, mammy, black buck) not only in cross-racial relationships, but in racialized conceptualizations of femininity, masculinity, and gender ideology as well.

In the meantime, with temporal migration and a geopolitical reconfiguration of the US borders in the second half of the nineteenth century, this racial/sexual divide was complicated further by eroding the racial binary in the racial/sexual divide already established through ownership of land and enslaved people. With the increased temporal arrival of Asian immigrant workers (in particular, Chinese men; see Nakano Glenn 2002), and after the 1848 US claiming of a large portion of Mexico and the presence of Mexicans in California (Almaguer 1994) and the Southwest, the racial understandings of citizenship made for a rocky set of legal battles, while immigration and settlement continued to make the United States, in particular the West, more Asian than before (Shah 2011; see also Zia 2000). In the case of immigrant men who wanted to achieve US citizenship, masculinity, not just sexuality and race, became a relevant factor. Significantly, while the last decades of the nineteenth century presented the hyper-masculinization of black men (read as being on the prowl) through processes of gendered migration and temporary employment in the United States, Asian men were portrayed as effeminate and asexual.

In 1898, when the Spanish-American war resulted in the conquering of Puerto Rico, the separation of Cuba from Spain, and the complicated relationship with the Philippines and other Pacific islands, the United States provoked a series of added migrations from the Caribbean and the Pacific, given this more complex geopolitical relationship. After this war, Manila, in the Philippines, became for many a place for temporary employment as a means to (eventually) migrate to the United States (Shah 2011). Although Cubans and Puerto Ricans were politically aligned in New York City during the late part of the nineteenth century, the Spanish-American war produced different readings of the two Caribbean countries, with Puerto Rico inherently associated with the United States (for more on Cubans' racial and sexual readings in the nineteenth and twentieth centuries, see the magnificent 2017 book by Mirabal). The beginning of the twentieth century saw increased militarization internationally, which also meant that further power relations with many Global South countries were solidified.[7]

There was an increase in Puerto Rican migration to the United States during the first half of the twentieth century (Vázquez-Hernández 2017; Whalen 2001), and in African Americans moving from the South to the North and the West (Ferguson 2004) – this after the official granting of US citizenship to Puerto Ricans (and their almost immediate draft into World War I). These migrations (and militarization across the board) increased interracial interactions, and challenged in significant ways the status quo that perpetuates a gender/sexual and racial purity ideology. The use of racial categories was subjective and related to aspects of citizenship and class, not just race; there was also elasticity for some groups – Mexicans, for instance, were considered a race in the 1930 Census, later on returning to a different nomenclature (Nobles 2000). (Incidentally, like Cuba and like African Americans in the United States, Mexico also produced racial discourses in their late nineteenth-century and early twentieth-century literature in response to the expansion of the United States; see Luis-Brown 2008.) During the last decades of the nineteenth century and the first decades of the twentieth, the social mobility of race and class was tested constantly; these swings also caused commotion within the realms of erotic labor and sexual desire (McClintock 1992, 1995).

The civil rights efforts of the mid-1960s also resulted in challenges to the status quo. A consciousness-raising around equal rights for black people invigorated a challenge to the law and the imposition of segregated spaces. The revision of immigration laws in 1965 initiated the arrival of large numbers of migrants (from Latin American and Asian countries in particular), which further cemented a more complex set of social–racial interactions. The following decades changed the (primarily) black/white racial binary that had marked much of the racial/sexual negotiations. By the late twentieth century, many social spaces, including schools and places of employment, were no longer racially homogeneous. (Unlike the melting pot assimilationist project earlier in the century, the end of the century marked a distinct difference and attempt to celebrate people's places of origin, race, and other social markers.) As issues pertaining to gender and sexuality came to the fore, these social spaces carried the legacy of racial conflict from years prior, while simultaneously hosting newly growing tensions relative to other axes of identity. For example, movies such as *West Side Story*, early on, and later *Do the Right Thing*, became stories about gender and sexuality, not just tensions or mixings of race and nationality. The intermingling of different nationalities and races meant a sexual and reproductive (and thus, social) threat to USAmerican society's racial-normative order. Citizenry (literal and symbolic) started to be heavily contested through people's relationship to the nation-state and the land (Brandzel 2016), to language (Urciuoli 1996), and even to notions of Latinas/os as inherently (and only as undocumented) immigrants (Chavez 2013).

The last decades of the twentieth century and the beginning of the twenty-first century have shown an even more complex relationship of racial groups, with the events of September 11, 2001, namely, the attacks attributed to al-Qaeda that destroyed the Twin Towers in New York City. The US response to these attacks was to begin wars against several countries, with an increased stigmatization of Arabs, Muslims, Middle Easterners, and South Asians (a disparate group of peoples whose range of ethno-racial, religious, and geographical differences do not merit profiling). But the fusion of sexuality and race in anti-Muslim portrayals as "monster-terrorist-fags" (Puar and Rai 2002) by the US military post-9/11 demonstrates the power of racialized sexualities and racism.

Studying sexuality and race

While this book is written by three sociologists, and many of the sources we cite are from the social sciences, we approach the study of these elements of structured forms of power through an interdisciplinary lens. This multidisciplinary approach prompts us to map our view of the fields that influence this book and to delineate the uneven influence of the fields of study we depend on. While the humanities and social sciences have been the primary fields examining this interaction between race and sexuality as a topic of analysis, their work on these connections has been unequal. Race and sexuality are often not linked in productively analytical ways in the social sciences but are often more connected (and productively so) in the humanities (important exceptions to mention, at a minimum, include Joane Nagel's *Race, Ethnicity, and Sexuality: Intimate Intersections, Forbidden Frontiers*; Roderick Ferguson's *Aberrations in Black: Toward a Queer of Color Critique*; Patricia Hill Collins's *Black Sexual Politics*; and Cathy Cohen's *The Boundaries of Blackness: AIDS and the Breakdown of Black Politics*). For the social sciences, feminist studies and black studies have operated implicitly as distinct fields – with black studies mainly focusing on race and feminist studies mainly focusing on gender – until intersectionality emerged.

As we discuss more fully in chapter 1, intersectionality – the tripartite of race, class, and gender – was a central analytical framework for understanding social locations – an individual's or group's placement in the social world – excluding other markers (and lenses) as potentially productive elements of social analysis. In fields such as sexuality and queer studies, the linkages to thinking about this tripartite are still seldom evidenced – the dearth of queer theoretical scholarship addressing these as interlocked forms of regulation has only been redressed in the last few years, given the newer waves of queer migration, queer diasporas, queer-of-color critiques, and a new queer cultural studies lens.

The humanities, on the other hand, have more actively produced scholarship that views race, gender, and sexuality in inherently interconnected ways. As a case in point, we follow in the footsteps of Kitch's *The Specter of Sex: Gendered Foundations of Racial Formation in the United States* (2009), which foregrounds a gendered lens as an analytic in race and racial formations. With strong undertones of a gendered sexualities analysis, Kitch's book centers "racial discourse as a *consistent historical analytic*; that is, in terms of the persistent use of gendered norms and judgments about appropriate or inappropriate gender standards to describe, classify, and stratify racial groups" (2009: 1). Kitch's work explores, through a historical lens, the intertwined processes through which racial formation becomes gendered, and shows how a genealogy of cultural norms developed. More specifically, Kitch demonstrates how, even as racial systems became elastic to accommodate newer racial groups and categories, there remained a gendered structure that was enacted through a set of specific variables, which she explores: bodies, blood, and citizenship. The inherent evaluation of approaches to gender that were read as racially deficient or successful is at the core of the book's historical analysis.

Other work in the humanities (some already mentioned) has also documented the interconnectivities of race and sexuality. McClintock (1995), Somerville (2000), and Smith (2005) have shown historically how colonialism, slavery, and genocide have shaped the racial and sexual formations of society in inter-articulated ways. Ross (2004) documents how same-sex sexuality is constitutive of the historical construction of black manhood, and Johnson (2008) records oral histories from black gay men in the South to challenge regional stereotypes about people in the South and to recover untold stories about men of color building sexual relationships with each other. Likewise, Muñoz's (1999) *Disidentifications* turns to queer people of color to theorize how minoritarian subjects work both within and against dominant structures and discourses in order to make space in the world (we discuss queer-of-color studies further in chapter 1).

Standing on the shoulders of some of these giants, this book delves into questions of the interrelation of aspects of sexuality and race as intrinsically inseparable elements constitutive of the social organization of our contemporary world. It does so by treating race and sexuality, together, as a critical lens through which to understand social arrangements and hierarchies, and the resulting sociocultural readings of difference. Our book connects these areas of study and lived experiences in ways that aim to loop back into black feminist thought, other feminists-of-color theorizing, and other linkages of sexed, sexualized, and racial matters. While race and sexuality have historically been associated with the biological, we treat these matters as culturally and socially produced and, as Somerville (2000) would argue, as intrinsically related moments that touched each other (in the case of *Queering the Color Line*, around the end of the nineteenth century, when homosexuality was emerging as a category, while a strong hold on the black/white racial binary was being solidified). In doing so, we interrogate the rigidity of constructions not only of race but of gender and sexuality as well. This notion of cultural and social production spans the cross-cultural, through which it becomes evident that what essentially counts as race or sexuality and the ways those things are discussed varies across time and space.

To fully contextualize the relationship between race and sexuality, we include historical examples that illustrate the interconnected relationship between the two. Racial and sexual formations are discussed in terms of the Chinese Exclusion Act, the war on terrorism, and various examples of the treatment of Global South countries throughout the nineteenth and twentieth centuries. We use frameworks that trace fields of study in social scientific and humanities studies; from sexuality and ethnic studies to intersectionality, to an understanding of mutually constitutive, or inter-articulation-based analyses. This approach is informed by sociology of sexuality, critical race studies, queer theory, queer-of-color critique, queer diaspora/migrations, transgender studies, transnational and postcolonial feminism, and intersectionality.

Chapter overview

This book hails a newer understanding of how these raced readings (as in the "welfare queen," or the hypersexual and reproductively active Latina teenager) are sexualized, and how sexualized readings (such as gayness being systematically produced as male and white, and homophobia most often imagined to happen in non-white communities) are always already raced. We move beyond the media-driven aspect of representation into a structural, discursive, and even an everyday level of analysis. The chapters you are about to read speak to lived experiences relative to sexuality and race, especially their intertwining constitution. The following chapters also speak to the institutions and systems that perpetuate the racial and sexual hierarchies ingrained in many societies today, but which were not established recently (indeed, it is the inheritance of these systems, in our view, that solidifies their impact today).

Part I brings together two conceptual chapters that discuss, as two sides of the same coin, the systems that operate to make race and sexuality so compatible in these social and cultural readings, as well as the interactional level of experience – the mundane – in the connection of these two axes of power. Through critical theorists and a review of relevant literature, chapter 1 articulates the racial system that distinguishes ethno-racial categories both historically and, in present times, with an eye for the discursive strategies of demarcating said racial system's hierarchical structure. The discussion also includes processes of sexualization as a way of understanding the role of sexual systems and gendered sexualities in conjunction with an ethno-racial analysis. The chapter contributes to the discussion by addressing the debates of the inclusion and exclusion of sexualities from the tripartite of intersectionality (race, class, and gender), as well as discussing embodiment and racialized sexualities.

Chapter 2 outlines the everyday accomplishment of these arrangements of racialized sexualities. This chapter combines the discussion about racial and sexual stereotypes in order to talk back to the systems in place by showing the centrality of whiteness, as well as heterosexism and homonormativity, in producing individualized notions of choice in race and sexuality biases. In this chapter, we seek to dismantle some of the recent neoliberal notions of racial and sexual discrimination as being about personal choice, especially with reference to dating preferences. We also think through "coming out" strategies and their relation to race and sexuality.

Part II of the book brings together three different case studies to show what we articulate as racialized sexualities and sexualized readings of race. Chapter 3 centers racialized sexualization in transnational human rights, where we examine the processes of sexualization rooted in the imaginaries of the Global South. We define transnational migration as the movement of individuals between countries and continents, which facilitates a complex constellation of networks and relationships between countries of origin and new countries. We situate migration in the relationship between the Global North and the Global South. These terms evolved in postcolonial studies to contextualize the relationship between countries in the West (otherwise known as the Global North) which possess a history of colonization and imperialism relative to Global South countries, which are the developing nations. By noting the inter-articulated nature of race and sexuality in a transnational context, we uncover the linkages between presumed victimhood on behalf of the Global South and its relationship to the imperialism and colonization of the West.

In chapter 4, we spotlight the relationship between race and sex work through various examples of sexual labor. In this chapter, we elucidate the interconnected nature of sexual fantasy imaginaries, specifically those enacted in various forms of erotic labor, to show how, for women of color, the limited availability of such imaginaries results in differential material realities as a result of participating in sexual labor. Discourses on erotic labor are owed to feminist interventions within the subfield, which received increased attention during the "sex wars" of the 1970s and 1980s.

Chapter 5 offers a timely review of the relationship between sexualities and migration, through which we uncover the multiple ways in which immigration and the mainstream portrayal of migrants in the Global North reflect problematic stereotypes rooted in the racist pathologizing of migrants as brown "Others." This chapter also evokes a historical view of sexuality and race in terms of gendered readings of Asianness, and the regulation of femininity (and in some ways, sexuality) through racial difference.

Lastly, the conclusion offers a revisitation of the major themes discussed throughout the text. Through this revisitation, we link the myriad areas implicated by racialized sexualities to demonstrate their inextricability from our daily lives. This book centers on the many ways in which racialized sexualities are communicated through what are understood as distinct experiences, including migration, sex work, and transnational human rights. By highlighting the shared significance of race and sexuality throughout all of these processes, we aim to demonstrate its power to constantly shape our experiences and realities in tangible ways.

While we cannot discuss every one of the influential texts, nor engage in all discussions that pertain to the topic of racialized sexualities, we aim to offer a foundational premise from which to build and form more scholarship. In a way, this book serves as a formulation of an argument that will endure in future arguments – whether in the social sciences, the humanities, or other interdisciplinary fields – so that the scholarship on race and sexuality continues to evolve into a study of sexualities that are often, if not already, racialized. From the introduction to the conclusion, we have considered race and sexuality as separate categories, then united them through an articulation of something more – what we call racialized sexualities. These are both everyday arguments, and subtle and complex ones – as the fabric of the social world. We expect that, in reading through these pages, you will consider and evaluate your own knowledge of cases of racialized sexualities in order to further show how race and sexuality are intertwined. Waking those examples up, and putting them in conversation with our case studies, is a crucial endeavor of thinking anew. We welcome you to thinking, analyzing, and writing on these topics with us.

PART I

Discourses of Race/Sexuality

1

Two Systems Operating Synchronously

In August of 2016, Kimberlé William Crenshaw offered a presentation at the American Sociological Association's annual meeting, entitled "Rethinking Social Movements: Can Changing the Conversation Change the World?". Crenshaw's intervention aligned with her decades-old work on critical race theory. Charlene Carruthers and Mariame Kaba, feminist and queer activists involved in Black Youth Project 100 and movement-building work against police brutality across the country, accompanied Crenshaw during this presentation. Alongside these activists, Crenshaw's focus was on her most recent project that makes visible the often hidden violence faced by black women and her campaign entitled #SayHerName. Crenshaw notes in this and other presentations how the Black Lives Matter visibility in the media tends to foreground the lives of (cisgender) black men, to the detriment of as many (if not more) women of color facing violence and death at the hands of police. The invisibility of gender violence (faced, every day, by cisgender and transgender women of color) in the women's interactions with police – as an extension of the gendered raced state violence faced by all women of color – provoked Crenshaw's focus on #SayHerName as an extension of her intersectionality work from the late 1980s and early 1990s. However, sexuality is often left without articulation in this work on gendered and racialized violence. More precisely, the inherently gendered

and sexualized violence faced by transgender women –
for breaking gendered and sex expectations, for embodying what is stereotyped as hypersexualized bodies that are
also commodified and placed on a sexualized gendered
market – merits as much attention as the ability to connect
#SayHerName to queer and sexuality-specific racialized
work (which the other activists-scholars more clearly did).[1]

As noted in the introduction, *racialized sexualities* is a
new area of study that is influenced by sociology, anthropology, history, American Studies, queer studies, feminist and
gender studies, critical race theory, literary studies, English,
rhetoric, political science, and geography. Our purpose in
this book is to advance a more focused understanding of the
notion that racialization is always already sexual, and sexualization is always already raced. How these categories are
mutually co-constituted is in many ways the purpose of this
chapter. We delve into the various theoretical approaches
and conceptual discussions on the topic, as well as interrogate the tenets of some of their propositions. Race and sexuality as mutually constituted is something that scholars in
the field of the queer-of-color critique (Cohen 1997; Reddy
1998; Muñoz 1999; Ferguson 2004) have already argued.
Some of these arguments are based upon women-of-color
feminism – mainly lesbians of color – who articulated how
gender, sexuality, race, and class are interconnected (Moraga
and Anzaldúa 1981; Lorde 1984; Barbara Smith, Demita
Frazier, and all of the other authors of the Combahee River
Collective Statement 1977).[2] More recently, queer theoretical
formulations of race and sexuality, with the work of scholars
such as Manalansan IV (2003), Guzmán (2006), Decena
(2011), and Pérez (2015), emerged as both support for, as
well as a challenge to, some feminist and gender studies
scholarship. In this and other chapters we approach this
theoretical and conceptual discussion as a scaffolding of
layers that will, eventually, illustrate the connections between
these fields of study, as well as how the notion of racialized
sexualities differs from these other scholarly arenas. Whereas

the introduction portrayed works at the disciplinary level, in this chapter, we embrace critiques, conceptual approaches, and contributions to knowledge production from smaller (non-disciplinary) projects, as well as interdisciplinarily.

Notice that, in our opening vignette, Crenshaw, a lawyer, is speaking at a sociology conference and is returning to intersectionality – a term she coined – and to the conceptual paradigm of exploring the place of women of color in feminist and race studies. We also frame the chapter with Crenshaw's intervention as it serves a dual purpose: it allows for the introduction of one of the topics we discuss in this chapter – intersectionality – while also breaking away from disciplinary structures (sociology, anthropology) and into a field of study with more specificity. But Crenshaw's appearance among a panel of activist women of color also introduces a break with the typical academic/activist binary so many of us operate in. Crenshaw and her fellow panelists draw attention to the lack of state intervention in the violence experienced by women of color. Crenshaw weaves together this structural phenomenon with the interpersonal by insisting on naming the axes of power that contribute to the lack of attention such events receive. By deliberately naming the perpetuation of structural violence (and subsequent invisibility) experienced by women of color, Crenshaw lays bare how the politics of invisibility are embedded in racialized and gendered discourses.

Thus we begin chapter 1 by discussing the different conceptualizations of race and how historical moments, structures, and processes impact racial formations. We focus in on main contributors to critical race theory, as well as the criticisms of some omissions from these theories. We also think through some potential (and current) expansions of such work. We then move to scholarship on sexuality using the very same structure, and addressing the connection between feminist and gender studies and queer theoretical formulations. In these two sections, we reveal how sexuality is often erased or invisible in how most people conceptualize racial formations, and we think through the implications of previous theorizing of race without thinking about sexuality. We then move to think about how sexuality and sexualization are conceptualized, and also interrogate the absence of race in these conceptualizations. We discuss the implications around the invisibility of race in discussions of sexual formations and also the tension created by including sexuality within an intersectional analysis – an important focus in the latter part of this chapter. We conclude chapter 1 by thinking through the academic, social, political, and cultural stakes of imagining sexuality and race as mutually exclusive analytical concepts versus co-constitutive social formations.

In the end, this chapter illuminates the conceptualization and utility of discursive practices in order to rethink the relationship of race and sexuality, in ways that will inform the next chapter, which focuses on lived experiences. Because we treat racialization and sexualization as discursive practices that have to be continually untangled and produced as distinctive, on and off the same grid, this conceptual chapter oscillates between earlier discussions by feminist and gender studies and racial formation theory, then delves into sexuality and queer theory in order to discuss intersectionality. Indeed, as we will show, we see both race and sexuality operating in and through each other all the time, so that racialization is not just about race and sexualization is not just about sexualities, although they are often continuously produced as supposedly being distinctive.

Race systems: the deployment of an ideology of raced beings

Conceptually, and building off the definitions and historical context provided in the introduction, this section expands on our understandings of race, racial formations, and racialization. To begin, the history of the United States is rooted in genocide, slavery, and the imperial foundation of the thirteen colonies' project of "manifest destiny" (a doctrine that alluded to the inherent and unstoppable urge to conquer all land west and south of the colonies). Colonial encounters acted as the foundation of the distribution of wealth; colonizers marginalized and dehumanized Native Americans and enslaved African peoples, and established the inherited systemic disadvantages – measured by resources such as land and freedom – that benefited white people over the rest. These historical processes of racial formation are an important historical point of departure. These power encounters that enforced labor and control, along with subhuman treatment, became part of the early racializing practices of domination that marked certain groups of people as inferior. (In Marxist language, the owners of the means of production controlled the free movement of, and threatened to assault and kill, those who became the enslaved workers producing the goods.) Those processes of demarcating all African enslaved peoples as black and forcing Native Americans off the radar and into imagined "nations within the nation" took decades to solidify. These same processes also signified white people as those who had access to and controlled the resources. Under the continuous expansion of the land by the United States, exploitation became the form of sustaining large quantities of production of buildings, of processing food and raw material, and the overall advancement of resource accumulation for those who became understood as white. The American Civil War began to map out a series of historical interventions to change the treatment of African Americans, but it would take another century for the actual implementation of civil rights (see Kibria, Bowman, and O'Leary 2014).

In the project of "manifest destiny," and the expansion of the wealth and power of the United States, the solidification of whiteness, as one extreme, and its counterpart, blackness, became the solid stones on which the country was built. This history haunts white people in the United States today, even when there are dismissive strategies and forms of rewriting history (people in the United States may recall the 2015 discussion about a high-school textbook produced by the publisher McGraw-Hill Education – one of the biggest textbook suppliers to the country – that discussed African enslaved people as "workers")[3] or other strategies of deflection that take place in order to avoid the historical structural violence and internal genocide of African enslaved peoples and Native Americans.

Omi and Winant's *Racial Formation in the United States* (1986, 1994, 2015) is squarely located at the center of this chapter in terms of thinking about the history of the United States, the forcefulness of the racial system, racial categories, and processes of racialization and nation-building. In particular, their conceptualization of racial formation theory as the mechanism through which racial categories were and are "created, inhabited, transformed and destroyed" (1994: 55) serves our framing of this chapter. Racial formation theory ties together the historical processes of racialization with the understandings of race. *Racial Formation* continues to influence these discussions, especially as we think about a notion of a "post-racial" society – a myth that continues to be enacted by multiple streams of conservatism and some forms of liberalism to dismantle denunciations of racism and discrimination. In this post-racial society, a social justice project gets rebranded as a "diversity" framework based on "inclusion" and "difference" – without bringing power into these discussions.

The twenty-first century brought a set of challenges to this black/white binary that had been so ingrained in the USAmerican imaginary of race. This obstinate binary could also be seen in the so-called "race relations" (Steinberg 2007) that arrived with multiculturalism, which accompanied us until the end of the twentieth century. Indeed, until the Twin Towers attack on September 11, 2001, the black/white binary still ruled the racial landscape in the USAmerican imaginary. This black/white binary was intact in spite of the 1965 immigration law changes that opened the doors to millions of immigrants who, according to Steinberg, were seen as the "new ethnics." However, when we insert 9/11 into conversations about racialization of Arabs/South Asians/Middle Easterners, and those (of any ethno-racial background) who are Muslim, we are not talking about immigration – and culture – but of groups associated with immigrant communities that have been racialized in powerful enough ways so as to authorize black and Latina/o people to endorse the surveil and register practices of those most targeted (Ahmad 2002). Historical discussions of racial classifications and the subjective meaning of race (for instance, the use of the documentary *Race: The Power of an Illusion, The House We Live In*) are important, but changes in the structural view of who becomes part of the groups at the "bottom" of the social-racial ladder (such as how 9/11 altered racial formations and meanings) are necessary.

Scholars have advanced the initial theoretical mapping and development of central concepts (such as racial formation and racialization) by pointing to the blind spots in Omi and Winant's theoretical contributions in terms of gender and sexuality (just as earlier scholars debated the saliency and centrality of class versus race – in particular, liberal thinking that it is not about race, but class), and what ultimately is foregrounded. For instance, the polarizing way in which the two (whiteness and blackness) were never to meet (literally, as in public space, and figuratively, as in interracial eroticism) was structured around ideas of access through gender and sexuality (e.g., anti-miscegenation laws). Likewise, African enslaved peoples were unable to sustain hegemonic ideas of familial structures, furthering experiences of domination and of dehumanizing them. Black women were often raped by their owners, and black men were feared because of the stereotypical perception of their being "on the prowl" and having the potential to emasculate white men (Davis 1981; Collins 2004). The scholars whose work challenges the racial lens think about the impact that race and sexuality have in the social imaginary of figures such as the "welfare queen" – as associated with African-American women (Kandaswamy 2012) and with the simplifying of feminist and queer efforts to counter some of these issues during the decades of the 1960s through the 1980s – at the very same time that Omi and Winant explored their racial formation theory (Ferguson 2012). Yet, historically, this work had not been connected in the fields of intersectionality, critical race theory, black feminist thought, or Latina/o scholarship; much less critical masculinity studies, queer theory, or queer-of-color critique. Until the Combahee River Collective, Moraga and Anzaldúa's work, and others connecting the two, the dearth of such conceptual crossings was only superceded by activists and artists on the fringes of academic work. But between the 1960s and into the 1980s, issues of same-sex rights and black civil rights were often explicitly managed through different lenses and by different actors in and outside academia.

Today, racialization processes, far from being about race as fixed or essential or biological, are being elucidated through their discursive lens (although one understands the genesis of racialization through bodies, hair texture, and skin color, racialization has moved away from the body and essential black/white binaries and onto social readings of perceived threat). "Doing" race does not only occur through phenotype, physical differences, but through religion, ethnicity, nation, sexuality, and so forth. Our point is that an evolution from embodied senses of racialization to structural enactments of racialization has occurred – and that one extends the others.

The (mis)uses of the cultural and ethnic vis-à-vis the racial is the closing aspect for this section – one that allows for our discussion to move, from race as oppositional to race as relational. While ethnic is often used in Europe to speak to national groups of people who have settled in certain host countries, we differentiate that term as used in the United States, which is about the diluted discussion of the racial through the image of the ethnic. Such reduction of racial discrimination, prejudice, and racism to ethnic groups and the ethnicization of racial difference prevent us from identifying a racial sexualization. Put another way, if our social lens/gaze is clouded by "ethnic" or "cultural" difference, we fail to see inequalities based on power relations and structures operating through the ethnic gaze.

The discussion of ethno-racial thus far has not extended to whiteness, which is often produced and deployed (through its omnipresence) as *lacking.* In his first essay on the topic, "Feeling Brown" (2000), José Esteban Muñoz, a performance studies queer theorist, moved the paradigm of racial difference and an oppositional binary to notions of race as relational. When whiteness is presented as devoid of culture, and yet results in culturally consuming the Other (hooks 1992), whiteness is both a racial agent but becomes invisible (and overarching). Muñoz theorizes a move away from Hispanic and Latina/o, as categories that stay within the ethnic and the racial, and onto brownness as a way of being (drawing from Raymond Williams's "structures of feeling," exploring the work of affective responses). For Muñoz, when Latinas/os such as Jennifer López or Marc Anthony are the Latina/o images that circulate, then a notion of Latinas/os as a group is created. When that notion is juxtaposed to whiteness in the USAmerican imaginary, it is not that Latinas/os such as Jennifer López or Marc Anthony are spicy, excessive, or exaggerated, but that white people are seen, in comparison, as lacking a production of affective responses vis-à-vis that imagery of Latinidad. This notion of race as relational informs debates about racialization for the study of its linkages with sexuality. Indeed, in Muñoz's work, it is queer and gender expansive Latina/o/x, black, Asian, and multiracial people who invoke a utopic space. The excessive sense of identification on both racial and sexual accounts signals the importance of taking both elements/sides of this equation equally seriously in order to produce an argument that is about the constitution of the sexualized and racialized through the (invisible) center (of whiteness and, as an extension, heterosexuality as norms).

The next section begins to illustrate the discursive aspects of sexuality by expanding on the previous discussion of racialization, but alongside the history of sexuality and sexual formations, gender studies, and queer theory.

Sexuality, sexualization, and gender and sexual norms

Like race, sexuality has a long history of being managed and regulated through agents of social control – in sexuality's case, religion and church as an institution, as well as psychiatry, medicine, and the social sciences (Foucault 1978 [1976]). This management and regulation is part of what we refer to as sexual formation – the historical placement of certain forms of sexuality and sexual identity in the foreground, while others are conspicuously absent. Today's social organization of sexuality is varied and open to several models of experience, but that has not always been the case. Furthermore, forceful deployments aimed at eliminating any kind of sexual variance in the past were as much about the regulation of crossing racial/sexual lines as they were about sexual activity and sexual identification.

Since the eighteenth and nineteenth centuries, discussions of sexuality have taken place through the lens of gender inversion. The actual categorizations of (first) homo- then heterosexual nomenclatures emerged in the late nineteenth century (Katz 2005) but they were not based on sexual attraction toward members of a different gender altogether – they were about gender inversion in a person's own sense of self. The subjective meaning of being a gay man or a lesbian woman, or even assuming a heterosexual identity, did not materialize until the twentieth century (D'Emilio 1993; Chauncey 1994). Even by the mid-twentieth century, and in spite of the advancement of a homophile movement, readings based on sexual behavior and attraction were elements resisted by people whose social organization was centered on a heterosexual way of life (see Humphreys 1970; for a different argument on the disentangled readings of sexual activity and a heterosexual sexual identity, see Ward 2015).

The literature on sexual formations is sometimes useful, given the normative and controlling images of a straight state (Canaday 2009) where heterosexual and citizen have been, historically, one and the same. Sexual formations, like racial formations, are about the processes of control – in this case, of any visibility outside the norm – in ways that mask the power relations involved in normalizing people. Yet a lot of the history of sexuality studies has inherently sustained non-normative sexualities as white, and cultures of resistance to such non-normativity as non-white (and homophobic). For instance, the invisibility of various racial groups in sex work research (refer to Frank 2002; Bernstein 2007; Chapkis 1997) fosters a similar characterization – more recent work has troubled those assumptions (Maia 2012; Miller-Young 2014; Brooks 2011; Jones 2015). Similarly, comparisons between marriage and issues of race and sexuality fail to be as congruent as social movement efforts might like them to be (Cahill 2005; but especially Reddy 2011). In sum, while structural issues of race and sexuality cross currents, they are by no means always analogous to one another.

Because sexualization should be understood as a process (instead of being fixed), and as a discursive effect instead of an essentialist fact (as in the clichéd sense of gay and lesbian people having been "born this way"), the power relations embedded in sexuality need to be critiqued. Sexuality does not only occur through the skin and sexual acts, but in fact its interpellation happens through religion, ethnicity, nation, race, and so forth. We are sexual beings in a multitude of ways. In this chapter, and the next, we have wanted to denote the differences between embodied senses of becoming a sexual being versus structural enactments of sexuality. If care is not taken in making that distinction, normativity around sexuality, sexual formations, and the relationship to the state is simplified.

Sexualization, as the inherently imposed and reductionist reading of someone's sexuality, differs from our understanding of sexuality in four ways (American Psychological Association, cited in Egan 2014): it is the foregrounding of someone's sexuality (to the detriment of all of their other characteristics): (1) as their currency; (2) as the imposition of exclusive definitions of sexiness on someone based on physical attractiveness; (3) as sexual objectification that imposes a reading of oneself as a "thing;" and, lastly, (4) as the imposition of sexuality onto someone. To be sexualized is to carry (with that reading) connotations that vary from the animalistic to the primal (and devoid of reason since they are attitude-driven and not based on any rational assessment). Thus to be sexualized is not just to be dehumanized; it is also to be infantilized, minimized, reduced to body parts, and thus, like race, propping up the hierarchy.

The product of the institutions and structural arrangements noted earlier helped establish a heteronormative form of intelligibility, and a subsequent unintelligibility for those who did not abide by such norms. Those are norms that are interlocked with sexism and misogyny as parallel operating systems. Indeed, sexuality discussions often tend to be restricted to men – most often gay men serving as the "subject" of this imagined topic – even though most people have the capacity for sexual desire. In particular, discussions of female desire and sexuality are often absent in most analyses of sexuality, whether the topic is cisgender women – be they heterosexual, lesbian, or bisexual – or some other sexual identity. The primary reading of the discussions on women's sexuality is foregrounded by their gender. They become understood as mothers, not sexual women or women with desires; their reproductive capacity is perceived to be their main social status. Or their sexual identity is neutralized by the aforementioned male-dominated categories (lesbian women are spoken of as *gay* women, understood as part of an "umbrella" term for sexual minorities). Similarly, when "gay" or "woman" are spoken of, the gender of sexuality, or the sexuality within the gender, gets erased for lesbian women.

There are other ways in which sexualization is tied to social identity and is also relational: as noted before, sexualization and gender (e.g., when women are understood only to be valuable if "pretty") but also racial sexualization (e.g., Craig, *Sorry I Don't Dance*, where white men are presumed not to want to move), and in terms of complicating understandings of race/class (e.g., Wilkins, *Puerto Rican*

"*Wannabes*," where white heterosexual women interested in men of color perform a racialized Puerto Rican gendered expression in order to get themselves space within black/ Latina/o groups).

As noted in the opening vignette, sexualization also happens to transgender women, and their experiences of being both gendered and continuously hypersexualized impact a structural perception of them (e.g., stereotypes, stigma), as well as their lived experience. Transgender women of color in particular face specific charges with regard to their ability to operate outside a sex-work framework – in many countries they live within very challenging situations where the levels of engagement are through prostitution (often where such labor is not an actual choice). Speaking of a trans-inclusive lens merits attention to gender frameworks that have incorporated gender, gender and sexuality, gendered sexualities, and race and sexuality around trans people, and trans women in particular.

Scholars in a specific framework of ethnomethodology have considered the symbolic boundaries of gender expression and trans identity. Harold Garfinkel (1967) was one of the earlier scholars whose work explored the gendered and sexualized experiences of a specific case study, Agnes (for more on this, see also Kessler and McKenna 1978; for transgender within a social institution, see Risman 1982). In much of that scholarship, transgender people challenged a dual-sexed way of operating in the world. The ethnomethodological scholarship expanded to incorporate linguistic practices and analyses of experience. According to sociologists Candace West and Don H. Zimmerman (1987), gender is an activity or accomplishment (something people *do*), managing one's behaviors within everyday life. Gender is more than being a man or a woman; gender is also about how masculinities and femininities become embodied and enacted. However, within our everyday interactions of "doing gender," people often reify institutional arrangements of men as dominant and women as subordinate. Gender and gender inequality are partially constituted through interaction, and through our interactions gender becomes naturalized (West and Zimmerman 1987; see also Butler 1990). Key though to West and Zimmerman's formulation of doing gender is that people cannot avoid "doing gender," as other people are always holding us accountable for our gender enactments. As Butler (2004) later stated, gender and other categories such as sexuality are dispossessed possessions or modes of relation, present in society before we are born and shaping how we relate to others.

Gender scholarship, either from specific frameworks such as ethnomethodology or from other areas of analysis, intended to explore the hierarchical aspects of difference, not merely to denote such difference. For much of this gender scholarship, difference was inherently about power and thus not an innocent articulation. This notion of power becomes important in thinking about the role of "doing gender" and how scholars such as West and Fenstermarker expanded this lens to "doing difference" (1995). Part of the insistence in feminist and gender studies (from an array of areas and as different paradigms) has been the necessity to remind everyone that women, as a category of analysis, were often forgotten, in spite of the necessity to preserve a diversity of women's experiences. Any scholarship and activism that produces a reminder of or an awakening to these erasures – be they women with disabilities, cisgender black women, transgender and transsexual women, women engaged in sex work – is inherently feminist. But often much of this scholarship did not examine or articulate the co-constitutive ways in which gender and other modes of difference are produced by and through each other. That is, things like doing gender are already raced, sexualized, and classed, and the failure to capture these complexities of power, difference, and hierarchies does not account for the intricate interactional and structural ways that shape lived experiences and inequalities. The rise of intersectionality began to address some of these lacunas.

Understanding the interlocking fields of study before, and through, racialized sexualities

Feminist studies and gender studies interrogated the normativity of elements such as sex/gender roles, moving society to newer family/work configurations (and the distribution of the private/public spheres) with work and family as non-oppositional. The study of sexism and the institutional barriers that precluded society from eliminating gender inequality were also central to such studies. Sexuality studies emerged along a continuum of work that insisted on class, race, and sexuality as equally important markers of identity and experience (Moraga and Anzaldúa 1981; Hollibaugh and Moraga 2000), and, at the same time, an emergent gay and lesbian studies, portions of which resulted in the coining of queer theory (de Lauretis 1991). The fields became intertwined with Crenshaw's (1991) intersectionality framework, and then with the advancement of scholarly work on queer theory and race, within specialized areas – some of which have already been mentioned (such as the queer-of-color critique), and others like queer diasporas (Gopinath 2005; Manalansan IV 2003) and queer migrations (Luibhéid 2002; Cantú 2009).

Intersectionality, first with Crenshaw and then Patricia Hill Collins, established itself as a crucial framework for social scientific analysis. But it has not gone without challenges to the situated knowledge it produced. In Crenshaw's launching of the paradigm, we see black womanhood unapologetically as the central point of theorizing and analysis. Crenshaw's initial proposition noticed the inherent racism and sexism in the treatment of black women and the inability of institutions (the law was a concentrated object of analysis for her) to recognize and respond to these dimensions of social life and experience which were already connected for black women (Crenshaw 1991; see also Grzanka 2014). Thus intersectionality began to flourish from a grounded set of denunciations of discriminatory practices and a well-defined embodied set of lived experiences.

Critical race scholar Angela Davis (1981) also denounced the oppressions of these multiple axes of power and continues to do so today in terms of the prison industrial complex, although in conversation with immigrant rights, disability rights, and anti-normative queer rights, as did Barbara Smith, a member of the Combahee River Collective. Patricia Hill Collins, too, began to engage in the project of studying intersectionality and expanded its scope.

Collins, a sociologist, first published *Black Feminist Thought* in 1990 (reprinting a second edition in 2000). She then developed her arguments for racialized sexualities in *Black Sexual Politics* (2004), where the interplay of race and sexuality came to the forefront. She addressed the interlocked forms of oppression for African-American and black diasporic women, and how black women are particularly sexualized. Yet in an early chapter she introduces, as an example of someone's black embodiment, the performer/dancer/singer/actress Jennifer López ("J-Lo" was the artistic name she was using then) to denote her voluptuous buttocks as a sign of López's inherent sexualized blackness. Instead of opening up the notion of black sexual politics to incorporate other women of color, Collins circumscribes López's experience in a black diasporic lens, thus reifying the very same black/white racial binary through the processes of sexualization that Jennifer López goes through. Ironically, López and other women of color are not recognized within the framework of this new intersectional lens, circumscribed as it was by African-American women's experiences of oppression. Thus, while intersectionality may be of utility to the rethinking of racial formation and sexualization, we seek to further unpack the various positionalities and experiences of non-black women, expanding to trans women of color and other social locations.

Also, intersectionality still, at times, operates within heteronormative logics. Again, in *Black Sexual Politics*, Collins sees men on the "down low" as being gay or bisexual, not allowing for the possibility of black men who engage in same-sex sexual behaviors having a heterosexual identity (reinforcing a "one-drop rule" that if a man engages in any type of same-sex sexual behavior, then they cannot be heterosexual; see Guzmán 2006). Collins links her discussion of the "down low" to HIV/AIDS – a topic we explore and critique in the next chapter as being a neoliberal strategy of furthering the pathologization of black sexuality and masking the structural causes of HIV within black communities. That is, within this intersectional framework, certain non-heteronormative forms of black male sexualities are still pathologized through dominant white logics of black men being hypersexual and hyper-masculine.

Queer-of-color critique emerges to queer intersectionality and to bring sexuality to critical race studies and race to feminist and queer studies. In "Punks, Bulldaggers, and Welfare Queens," Cathy Cohen (1997) argues that feminist and queer scholarship must contend with how heterosexual norms do not privilege all heterosexuals; that is, heterosexual people are not a monolithic group (and some queer people experience privilege). For example, the figure of the "welfare queen," single parents, and even interracial relationships are also outside of the hegemonic heterosexual norms of society. In this regard, one must begin to think about how the existence of single mothers or "welfare queens" – racialized figures and stereotypes – may also be sites to challenge compulsory heterosexuality and heteronormativity.

Furthermore, in *Aberrations in Black*, Ferguson (2004) utilizes a queer-of-color analysis through his documentation of how nationalist ideologies, liberal ideologies, and sociological research all came together to maintain the white hetero-patriarchy. In one of his chapters, Ferguson turns to the Moynihan Report – a report by a sociologist who implied, perhaps inadvertently (and through a heteronormative, masculinist lens), that black families are in poverty because black women run the households and in the process emasculate their male partners. Moynihan calls for a reinscription of a patriarchal household within black families and communities as the solution to black poverty. Ferguson argues that Moynihan (along with the other sociologists, such as the

Chicago school of ethnography that Ferguson critiques) often assumed that patriarchy and heterosexuality were "natural" and right. In the mid-twentieth century, sociologists saw the social decay (e.g., non-heterosexual relationships, non-nuclear families) and social disorganization caused by capitalism within black and other communities of color as inherently bad. Instead of seeing these non-heterosexual and non-nuclear relationships as sites to critique larger structures of society, sociologists instead called for black communities to return to patriarchal, heterosexual family structures in order to end discrimination against them. In these instances, because black communities did not give in to compulsory heterosexuality (often because they could not, due to factors like poverty and incarceration that render relationships for people of color extremely tenuous), discrimination against people of color was justified. An understanding is needed of how heteronormativity is also used to support racial and class inequality alongside gender inequality. Therefore, a queer-of-color analysis calls for and shows how social formations and their resulting inequalities and constructions of social difference operate in and through the inter-articulations of gender, race, sexuality, and class.

Now the field of racialized sexualities addresses those complexities in various parts of the globe, engaging in colonial and diasporic lenses, engaging cisgender women, trans women of color, immigrants, and transnational groups of people. The scope of the fields of study influencing the newer racialized sexualities studies is still expanding, and our efforts in this book are a small step in that direction.

Conclusion

In closing, the importance of considering both race and sexuality together cannot be overstated. We have been thinking through how sexuality and race are often imagined as mutually exclusive analytical concepts, as in some applications of intersectionality, versus co-constitutive social formations, as in racialized sexualities. But these fields are not impermeable, and they continue to expand and relate to each other in more intimate ways.

While these concepts are not always variables with exactly the same levels of analysis, they provide us with a powerful analytics to see the connections of stereotypes, power, and prejudice. In the final analysis, what is lost when we ignore one or the other is the ability to provide a nuanced account of whatever social issue we want to explore. In this chapter, we have identified crucial aspects of racialization and sexualization that merit attention. For example, the fear of talking about race or racism in a "post-racial" era or denying the relevance of race in contexts that are racially mixed are aspects of the cross-over between the two elements that have to be overcome.

We find it necessary to insist on this relationship at a time where the hyper-visibility of racialization and sexualization is more evident than ever, as the following chapter will show.

2

Race and Sexualities in Everyday Life

In April of 2017, professional football player Aaron Josef Hernandez allegedly committed suicide while serving a life sentence for first-degree murder. Following the news, a lot of media attention (mostly from gossip columns, although *Newsweek*, and gay newspapers such as the *Washington Blade*, included coverage) produced a "hidden bisexual orientation" narrative as the cause for both his murder case, as well as his eventual suicide – some going so far as to note that Hernandez left a note to his "jail boyfriend" before committing suicide. Aaron, of Puerto Rican and Italian descent, was said to be fearful of the possibility that his sexuality would be publicly known; and that, combined with his ethno-racial heritage, this would amount to unbearable social stigma.

Stories such as this one reveal the media's obsession with promoting non-normative sexualities as shameful, and construct narratives of guilt and suicide based on these reasons. Bisexual people are often stereotyped as dangerous and hypersexual, whereby bisexuality is often seen as a "phase" but not a legitimate sexuality or identity (Callis 2013). While self-identified bisexual people have been openly so (to their families and friends, and to the media) in recent decades (partially working to dispel some stereotypes about bisexual people), the challenge posed to Hernandez's biography is one that is also raced – coming from Puerto Rican and Italian parents, his suicide may be more easily co-produced as a recognition that non-normative sexualities do not operate in the lives of people other than white people. Constructions of homophobia in communities of color, and of pride in white communities of being gay, lesbian, bisexual, transgender and/or queer, abound in white USAmerican narratives. For example, in 2008, voters in California elected Barack Obama to the presidency while also passing Proposition 8 – a ban on same-sex marriage. A dominant narrative that grew out of Proposition 8 was that people of color voted for this ban, even as (white) LGBT people voted for a black president. This discourse often erased the existence of LGBT people of color, while constructing people of color as homophobic, also erasing how US society as a whole is heteronormative and homophobic. This chapter will illustrate how the discursive practice of a socially shared agreement about these presumed silences is deployed, as both producers and consumers of media – an important social institution – enact a "common sense" narrative that is tacitly agreed upon and subsequently achieves traction (enough so that it makes this "common sense" knowledge float unquestioned). We seek to dismantle that perceived common sense with an analysis of the structural aspects of race and sexuality.

Thus, in this chapter, we move the discussion to show how racialized sexualities affect people's everyday lives. We reveal how the discursive and structural elements of society around race and sexualities produce certain raced sexual readings of particular bodies. We discuss how race-based sexual stereotyping shapes people's desires, as well as who is desired, and how people are desired in particular ways. We also illuminate how neoliberal discourses around "personal preference" justify people's discriminatory acts, masking the structural inequalities that shape these desires. From there, we explore how racial and sexual embodiments and their meanings can vary by context, and how the intersections of race and sexualities generate particular social inequalities for different groups of people. We conclude this chapter by thinking about the timely issue of "coming out" as an LGBT political strategy, and how race, ethnicity, and nationality can complicate and challenge this strategy.

Race, sexualities, and the quotidian

Bodies, individuals, and communities all experience structural and discursive elements of raced sexual readings; in turn, as members of society, people reinscribe those readings and categorizations. All bodies are raced, just as they are gendered and sexualized; however, their markings are given different meanings depending on the relational potentiality between them, the social context of bodies, acts, activities, and, overall, their social location versus established hierarchical structures. This chapter engages the linkages between a raced/sexualized (and often gendered and classed) body, or constituency, and the social systems that race/sexualize it. We begin with the commonplace or routine (the seemingly mundane, unscripted, or unmarked, set of experiences of being in the world) and move back and forth between those and a set of social systems that regulate the quotidian.

Following the discussion in the previous chapter, we engage with questions of being racialized (and existing within an ethno-racial system) and how this relates to sexualities at the micro/experiential levels. To say that someone (or something) is racialized is to recognize the perception of a behavior attributed to a person/group of people in ways that may create false perceptions of them *as representative of a group* (Omi and Winant 1994). Thus such a reading incorporates a particular value – a value that is never about that person, or that element, but about a community of people (hence, being racialized as a member of an ethno-racial minority group often carries stereotypes and stigmatizing messages of some sort). There are different types of racialization: religious, ethnic, gendered, sexual, and other forms of racialization. In the context of this chapter, gendered and sexual racializations are front and center. For instance, stereotypes that function to racialize black and Latina women on the basis of their sexuality, race, and gender include the imaginary of Latina women having multiple babies, when they are thought of as hyper-reproductive (García 2012) and the figure of the "welfare queen" in government policies (Bensonsmith 2005; Kandaswamy 2012; Schram 2005). These are but two examples of how Latina and black women are particularly racialized, on the basis of a combination of their sexuality, gender, and race. It is important to note that white people are racialized too, although the stigma, or sense of capital, given to each form of being racialized varies – not just in mainstream USAmerican contexts, but in subcultural spaces (for instance, being racialized as a "thug" may offer cachet to some men and women; for more on the latter, see Wilkins 2004).

We should not confuse ethnic and racial readings in this ethno-racial landscape. Being racialized and being ethnicized carry different connotations. To be ethnicized is to have a culturalized reading of one's self (or of one's food, clothing, accent, gendered being), which is often devoid of any significant political, social, or economic value. Ethnic use of clothing or language (as in Spanish folk songs) is seen as ethnicized, because, among other things, these readings are rendered innocent (Urciuoli 1996). However, scholars such as Grosfoguel (2004) have complicated the relationship between these two markers by signaling the porousness of both as "racialized ethnicities" or "ethnicized races." But to be racialized is to carry specific connotations about a group of people in ways that, at the least, create a specific orientation of such groups (for instance, all black people behave a particular way, or all Latinas/os are Mexican undocumented immigrants, because that's what we see in the news). At worst, this sustains stereotypes or perpetuates violence against such groups. Many USAmericans ethnicize people of color in order to avoid thinking of the hard reality of systematic racism in society, but they may quickly turn to racializing when historically biased norms of social order cues are threatened – voting for bilingual education, speaking a different language at work, or seeking citizenship and claiming the very same sense of Americanness.

Racialization at a local level is distinctively unique and cannot be simplified to national media soundbites of immigration and undocumented status. What racialization at the local level may mean, in a US context for instance, is that Californians may racialize Latin American immigrants as Mexican and Central American, and most often as undocumented, when in reality more than half of those who are identified as Latina/o or Latin American are residents or US citizens. Or people make assumptions that racialize as undocumented many Asian/Pacific Islander immigrants who are Chinese or Filipino, even though many in such groups have already (re)produced several generations in the region – thus creating a blurry confusion between those whom USAmericans racialize as immigrants and those who are actually new migrants to the country. If we take New York as another example of local racializations that clash with national imaginaries, we see how Latinas/os (including Puerto Ricans who are fourth- and fifth-generation migrants, a group of people who have been moving to NYC since the nineteenth century) are *still* considered (and called) "Spanish" folk by USAmericans, even though most Dominican, Colombian, and Mexican immigrants to NYC are far removed from those categorizations. And if we take the rest of the US southern border – Arizona, New Mexico, and Texas – we notice the critical racialization that Mexican Americans and other US-born Latinas/os go through, as they are often marked/racialized as "undocumented immigrants" by a USAmerican white group which is entitled, conservative, and a ruling group whose basis for hate is fear of the immigrant. Even though those they see are US citizens, their race becomes a target, in spite of their citizenship (and non-immigrant status). These slippages are important, as a lot of stereotyping flows from these readings of Otherness, when race and migration are tied together, yet remain unproblematized.

At the intimate and erotic level, race-based sexual stereotyping often casts black and (when mentioned) Native American men as hypersexual, Latinos as exotic "others," and Asian men as effeminate and asexual (see Wilson et al.

2009), while retaining whiteness as innocence – ever since the historical contrast made between black male slaves as hypersexual and predatory and white females as delicate but desiring of a perceived black male's sexual potency (see Kitch 2009). These stereotypes work to establish whiteness as the structuring mode of sexual propriety and to justify discrimination against people of color for failing to align with such standards (failing to align with them also makes them less desirable as partners). In the private sphere, as well as in erotic dancing and porn, (female) whiteness is understood as the basis of sexual patterns of desire, and white (female) bodies are given the advantage in embodying sexualized fantasies – bride, schoolgirl, and so forth – whereas women of color are reduced to sexualities framed as "animalistic" (Khan 2015). These stereotypes – which creep into the social imagination/omnipresent discourse of racialized desire – also affect the daily lives of people, especially as they try navigating dating and/or finding sexual partners.

At the present time, many white people may not want to date people of color because of these stereotypes, and (simultaneously) people of color often try to embody these stereotypes in order to be more desirable or give their racial minority status some sexual cachet (Guzmán 2006). Those who do engage in interracial relationships face judgment and suffer from tension within their relationships over issues such as negotiating where to live, where to school their kids, or even facing hostility when perceived as not being the parent (Steinbugler 2012; see also Katz Rothman 2005). These stereotypes erase heterogeneity among people of color, lumping them together in homogeneous categories to be culturally consumed, assumed to be on the prowl (and sexually violent), reduced merely to their genitals (Robinson and Vidal-Ortiz 2013), and/or simply ignored when interacting with other individuals (see Collins 2004; Han 2006a, 2010; Brooks 2010).

Neoliberalism shapes how race and sexualities are experienced today (see Holland 2012), so that "choice" and "individuality" are tenets of social organization, and thus a biased sexual-racial "preference" (apparent individual choice in dating and sexual hookups) is not read as racism (Robinson 2013, 2015). These "individualistic responsibility" frameworks are a part of larger neoliberal economic policies that have restructured the social through the retrenchment of social welfare programs and through widening economic inequality, all the while placing the burden of economic responsibility on the individual. This same discourse on individual responsibility influences people's discussions of their desires by talking about their "personal preferences," veiling the structural inequalities shaping these desires. Therefore, stereotypes of people of color's sexual behaviors and sexual health are seen as people of color's own moral failings. We hail these larger structural inequalities and discourses behind seemingly personal choices and turn the lens back onto the structures of being that influence people's interpersonal and intrapsychic erotic desires (see Guzmán 2006).

An example of how race-based sexual stereotypes and neoliberal discourses operate with regard to "personal preference" is online dating. The internet was believed by some to be a place where social inequalities could be done away with. Indeed, issues such as segregation could potentially disappear online, as people may interact with people of other races more online than they do offline. However, race-based sexual stereotypes still deeply impact online dating and sexual hookup interactions. In a study on Yahoo Personals, researchers found that white men often exclude black women as potential dating partners, and white women often exclude Asian men (Feliciano, Robnett, and Komaie 2009). In a different study on online dating, it was found that people often contact people of the same race as them and are also more likely to respond to people of the same race or to someone from a dominant racial group (Lin and Lundquist 2013). For multiracial daters, if they identify as part white, their chances of receiving a response on an online dating site improve (Curington, Lin, and Lundquist 2015). When online dating, gay men also often used "personal preference," though this discourse was adopted to mask cultural assumptions that gay men have of people of color and to justify gay men's preference for white men (Robinson 2015). Such systems even let people filter out someone based upon their race, exacerbating these notions of racial inequality and stereotyping within online dating.

Spotlight 2.1 Racialized Sexualities and the "Down Low"

The construction of the "down low" is a rich example with which to explore race-based sexual stereotypes and the ways in which race, sexuality, and gender intersect to pathologize certain forms of sexual contact and intimacy. In 2003, Benoit Denizet-Lewis – a white man – in his *New York Times* piece "Double Lives on the Down Low" brought the concept of the "down low" (DL) to national attention. In this piece, Denizet-Lewis depicts an underground world of black (and some Latino) men who identify as heterosexual and have wives or girlfriends, but who have sex with other men. In his portrayal of "DL" men, being gay is to be white and effeminate. "DL" men place their racial identity above all other identities, so to be black is to be masculine and heterosexual. Although Denizet-Lewis acknowledges that some black men openly identify as gay, he claims that most black men with same-sex desires and who engage in same-sex intimacy do not. Instead, these "secret lives" of men of color on the "down low" get linked to "unsafe" sex and rising HIV rates among people of color.

A year later, J. L. King released his memoir *On the Down Low*, in which he detailed his own sex life with men. King dedicates the book "to all the women whose health has been jeopardized and emotional state compromised by men living on the DL." Again, the "down low" is linked to the spread of disease, and women in relationships with men on the "DL" get depicted as passive victims. Similar to Denizet-Lewis's argument, men on the "down low" in King's account are married or date women because if they did not their community would label them as "fags" – a term that is perceived as stripping a black man of his masculinity (King 2004). King hoped that his memoir would inspire men on the "down low" to "come out," presuming that men on the "DL" are really gay or bisexual.

A year after King's memoir, Keith Boykin published *Beyond the Down Low.* In his book, Boykin (2005) challenges the media's construction of those on the "down low" as black, male, HIV-positive, in a relationship with a woman, but sleeping with other men. Boykin asserts that same-gender sexual activity among men happens between and across ethnic and racial lines; white men sleep with other men secretly as well, so why are white men not getting blamed for the spread of HIV/AIDS in the white community? For Boykin, the "down low" construction is a way for "white America" to pathologize black male sexuality. As Boykin asserts, there is no empirical evidence (there still is not) that the "down low" has contributed to the rise in HIV infections within black communities.

From these more popular discourses, two main lines of inquiry followed in scholarly research. First, what is the sexual identity of men on the "down low"? And, second, are "DL" men contributing to the rise of HIV? "Down low" men were seen as bisexually active (Agyemang 2007), as black masculine men having sex with other black masculine men (Phillips 2005), as gay, but using the label "down low" to negotiate their cultural contexts (Valera 2007), and as heterosexual men who have sex with each other but maintain heterosexual lives outside of their same-sex sexual contacts (González 2007). Although without empirical evidence, research also promulgated that men on the "down low" were spreading HIV throughout black communities (Valera 2007). One argument as to why black men are on the "down low" is that black communities are especially homophobic. Besides the lack of any empirical evidence for this claim, this statement is problematic in that it fails to explain how homophobia is pervasive throughout US society. Instead, this discourse about homophobia in the black community eclipses how poverty – a problem generated partially by structural racism – often underlies rising HIV rates in black communities, more so than men on the "down low" (Phillips 2005).

In effect, discourses about the "down low" have been used to pathologize same-sex sexual behavior among black (and Latino) men. This same-sex behavior is given a deviant label – the "down low" – and then seen as being engendered because of homophobia within black communities, giving rise to the increase in HIV rates within those communities (Han 2015). It bears repeating that there is no empirical evidence for either of these discourses.

Furthermore, research has shown that heterosexual white men are also on the "down low" (Robinson and Vidal-Ortiz 2013; Vidal-Ortiz and Robinson 2016) and engage in same-sex sexual encounters (Ward 2015; Silva 2017). Some white men may claim to be on the "down low" in order to try to attract black and Latino men (Vidal-Ortiz and Robinson 2016). Nonetheless, the fact that there are white men claiming to be on the "down low" challenges the notion that the "down low" is only a person-of-color phenomenon because of homophobia within communities of color (Robinson and Vidal-Ortiz 2013). It also unsettles the link between HIV and the "down low," as white men are engaging in the same types of behaviors yet HIV rates do not seem to be rising in the same ways. This fact points to the need to examine how poverty and discrimination may be the underlying causes of HIV in black and other communities of color, more so than individual sexual behaviors.

Moreover, whiteness and heterosexual white men get to experience their same-sex sexual encounters differently than black and Latino men. In *Not Gay: Sex Between Straight White Men*, Ward (2015) argues that heterosexual white men's engagements with one another uphold their whiteness, heterosexuality, and masculinity. Straight white men have been engaging in sexual encounters with each other for quite a while (e.g., in the military, in biker gangs, in fraternities); however, their same-sex sexual encounters never get pathologized or labeled as the "down low" or justified as happening because of homophobia within white communities or a cause of HIV within white communities. Instead, heterosexual white men get to engage in same-sex sexual behaviors as a way to further their investment in masculinity and heterosexuality. In effect, then, the "down low" is a discourse that relies on racialized sexual stereotypes about men of color being hypersexual and deviant which pathologize their same-sex sexual encounters in ways that do not apply to white men who do the same thing.

The multiple meanings of racial and sexual embodiment vary by context. For example, beauty norms within communities of color may vary, such that white hegemonic beauty norms like being skinny or stereotypically feminine (in particular white-American femininity standards) may not always apply. Although women of color have to contend with these hegemonic beauty standards, things such as being curvy may also be valued by some black and Latina women. Such hegemonic beauty norms may still shape certain practices (e.g., eyelid surgery, lightening skin treatment) based on ideological premises like colorism – discrimination based on one's skin color, whereby lighter skin is privileged over darker skin (Hunter 2005; Nakano Glenn 2009). Physical markers that are associated with the bodies of people of color are often seen as excessive, crude, or unattractive when whiteness is the standard – and these elements are gendered and sexualized (this is the case for cisgender *and* transgender women; Vidal-Ortiz 2014). When these features have been adopted by white (cisgender) women (i.e., lip injection, "Brazilian" butt lift, etc.), they take on a favorable meaning (Wilkins 2004). White women who embody these features are often seen as exotic and sexually desirable, whereas brown and black women embodying the same features are judged differently. The processes by which this appropriation occurs are ever-changing, meaning that different embodied features reach "trend status" at different points in time, demonstrating the transient nature of racialized desirability.

The intersections of race and sexualities also generate particular social and health inequalities. For example, according to the Centers for Disease Control and Prevention, black gay and bisexual men are more affected by HIV than any other group in the United States. Socioeconomic status can influence these disparities, as some black gay and bisexual men may have limited access to quality health care and disproportionately experience mass incarceration. Furthermore, black people develop sexual stories around HIV in order to understand how structural patterns interact and influence their sexual health and lives (Mackenzie 2013). Some black people trace the high rates of HIV within black communities back to the trauma of slavery and the medical experiments done on black people; that is, some black people see the high rates of HIV as another attempt by the state to try to marginalize and discriminate against black people and communities (Mackenzie 2013).

Sexual stigma and discrimination can shape how communities of color respond to and talk about certain sexual topics such as HIV. This stigma can negatively affect testing and seeking treatment. To preserve their privacy, people avoid going to HIV clinics (Lichtenstein 2003). Young women of color have recently carried the stigma of human papilloma virus (HPV) in the United States, and Latina teenagers in particular face challenges based on sexual education, reproductive choice, and teenage pregnancies (García 2012; Mann, Cardona, and Gómez 2015). Women of color also encounter structural barriers when it comes to reproductive health and are more likely to die during pregnancy compared with white women (Fiscella 2004).

This realm of reproductive health and the barriers that women of color face have played out in important ways within feminist movements. In *Women of Color and the Reproductive Rights Movement*, Nelson (2003) reveals how women of color in the United States and Puerto Rican feminists challenged white feminists to broaden their pro-abortion platform to cover a more expansive reproductive rights framework. White feminism (in Nelson's account, mainly the Redstockings) often only framed reproductive rights around choice of and access to abortion. Feminists of color challenged this narrow vision because women of color often did not even have the "choice" of an abortion because of other social constraints (e.g., poverty, lack of access to a living wage). Likewise, women of color were also dealing with issues of forced sterilization, the state often sterilizing women of color without their consent. Therefore, many white feminists often perceived sterilization as a voluntary procedure, while many women of color saw sterilization as state control of their bodies. Women of color pushed white feminists to pursue a more inclusive reproductive rights framework that would encompass sterilization and other social issues such as employment.

Likewise, women of color often have to deal with nationalist sentiments within their own communities – something again that white women do not have to contend with. During the 1960s and 1970s, black nationalists often wanted black women to keep bearing children in order to combat the perceived racial genocide of their community. Black women not only had to confront white women regarding expanding notions of reproductive rights, but they also had to challenge black men within their own communities about their bodily autonomy. Black women's reproductive experiences were qualitatively different to white women's experiences, and the call for a more inclusive reproductive framework was an outcome of feminists of color challenging both white feminists and black nationalist agendas (Nelson 2003).

Similarly, in *Conquest*, Andrea Smith (2005) also talks about the rape and forced sterilization of Native American women. In addition, Native American women have been medically experimented upon, and they have experienced the environmental degradation of their communities. This pollution of their land also affects Native American women's pregnancies and reproductive capabilities. Andrea Smith reveals how, alongside forced sterilization, issues like environmental racism are also acts of sexual violence on women's bodies and their reproductive health. She calls for doing away with a "pro-choice" framework around reproductive rights, considering this framework too individualistic and consumer-based. She also says that this "pro-choice" rhetoric completely disguises the fact that many women do not even have a "choice" in reproductive decisions. She calls for a more inclusive reproductive rights framework that confronts the many issues that women of color face, including rape, forced sterilization, genocide, and environmental degradation (Smith 2005).

These social inequalities generated through the intersections of race and sexualities are further exacerbated by the law. The criminalization of HIV "is one site in which anti-blackness, AIDS phobia, queer phobia and carceral violence converge" (Gossett 2014: 34). As both mass incarceration and the AIDS epidemic disproportionately affect black and Latina/o populations, the criminalization of HIV continues the surveillance of minority populations. For example, Nushawn Williams became a media example of how the politics around HIV criminalization plays out and impacts men of color. Williams was sentenced to prison in 1997, partially because he knowingly had HIV and had condomless sex with women. Williams's case ignited a media storm about whether HIV should be criminalized and if infecting someone deliberately with HIV should be seen as attempted murder. Within these discussions, Williams was seen as promiscuous and sexually out of control. Black men are often already stereotyped as hypersexual and, through Williams having HIV (and potentially infecting people), this stereotype was exacerbated by the media spectacle and the courts. Although Williams has served his sentence, he has still been prevented from leaving prison as he is considered a public health "risk" to society.

Outside of health and the law, race, ethnicity, and nationality can also shape "coming out" strategies and narratives as well as different responses to non-heterosexual behaviors and identities. "Coming out" is often depicted as the "authentic" way to be LGBT within US society. However, this construction of coming out of the closet ignores how different people navigate being LGBT, based on their social location and when and how they choose to disclose this information. That is, "coming out" and the closet are often seen as middle-class, white notions of experiencing one's sexual marginality (Ross 2005). Certain people and communities of color may not "come out" in the same ways that the (white) hegemonic gay narrative often requires of people who want to be "authentic" gay subjects (see Decena 2008; Acosta 2013). Some people of color may see no need to "come out" as they may believe their family and friends already know about their non-heterosexuality. For example, in his study on gay Dominican men in the United States, Decena (2011) shows how men tacitly negotiate being gay within their families without having to openly disclose their non-heterosexual identity. In challenging the "compulsory disclosure" that one is supposed to perform as an "authentic" gay subject, some gay men navigate their racial and sexual identities differently to the dominant paradigm. Some black gay men may see their racial and sexual identities as interlocking; other black gay men may perceive them as in opposition to each other. Yet others may base them on space and contexts (Hunter 2010). In effect, LGBT people of color are not a monolithic group and respond to "coming out" and being a racial and sexual minority in a variety of ways. To be clear, plenty of non-white non-heterosexual people "come out" and rejoice in identifying with such nomenclature; but the challenge is to manage what sociologists call the "master status" (i.e., the primary identifying status of a person) and the assumed contradiction of racial minority status with an LGBT identity – a challenge that somehow makes whiteness invisible in the process of coming out "while white." Likewise, some non-heterosexual people of color may see neither identity as a master status (Hunter 2010).

Conclusion

In the previous chapter and this one, we have moved discussions of racialized sexualities from theoretical and discursive levels to the everyday lived realities of people, the point being that how race and sexuality are operationalized as co-constitutive elements has concrete material and social lived consequences. Racialized sexualities affect dating and relationship formations, embodiment and desire, the criminalization and/or stereotyping of certain people's sex lives and behaviors, sexual health, and even "coming out" strategies. Our lives are influenced daily by the ways in which race and sexuality always operate simultaneously.

In the previous section of the book, we established a common language through key concepts, a core set of definitions, and reviews of critical, relevant literature; we also illustrated both disciplinary influences and more recent contributions as framed by newer fields of study, conveying the discursive, the social, the institutional, and the interpersonal. In the following three chapters, we turn to case studies – transnational human rights, sex work, and immigration – to explore the ways in which the discursive, the macrostructural, and everyday lived realities all shape how racialized sexualities influence these different areas.

PART II

Transnational, Local, and Global Sexual/Raced Messages

3

Racialized Sexualization in Transnational Human Rights

Coverage on world news often reveals a troubling dynamic which is quite foundational in processes of globalization and the transnational negotiations of human rights. In Europe, the United States of America, Australia, and other Global North countries, there is a flood of asylum cases of *people* whose right to *be* is diminished – be they lesbian women, gay men, bisexual people, transgender individuals (LGBT), or women whose rights to experience life as equal human beings are denied. There are of course some instances in which sociocultural, political, religious, and (often) legal mechanisms in the countries where applicants reside undermine their well-being as members of groups of people who have been categorized as being "at risk" of violence, rape (corrective or otherwise), torture, and death. Pressure on European countries to accept vast numbers of people means that regulations to "test" or "prove" whether someone is a member of the lesbian, gay, bisexual, or transgender communities (the term sexual minority is also applied) have been instituted, and only recently have asylum seekers won the right not to be judged on specific criteria proving their particular marginalized status (Smith 2014; for more on this process, see Peña 2007). Asylum seekers whose sexual and gender experiences are invalidated back "home" struggle to be treated as humans in the countries which, begrudgingly, grant them asylum (when they do), while in the process, their humanity is made more fragile (Bernini 2015). What news coverage does not present is the unbalanced, and often colonial/hierarchical/racialized, dynamics inherent in these cases of sexual orientation and gender (identity). The construction of western countries as advanced and progressive in terms of human rights is juxtaposed to countries that are portrayed as backward (Decena 2011); the latter group is read (signified) in marked racialized (and colonial) ways that are at the crux of this chapter's argument.

In the previous chapter, and as part of the first section of the book, we discussed, *a grosso modo*, the impact of racialized sexualities and gendering on everyday life as a strategy that allowed for understanding structures that operate in and through the body. In this chapter, we examine the ways in which the concepts of gender and sexuality are framed, utilized, and unevenly evaluated (what we later call deployed) within transnational human rights – in terms of such human rights' ideological underpinnings as well as their implementation as a homogeneous platform (what we hereon refer to as discourses). We thus propose to study the circulation not only of marked bodies but also of stigma, the devaluation of migrants, and the reorganization of Global North and South governments which supports a colonial/racial order through sexuality and gender in human rights at an international level. We focus on both gender and sexuality not only because they are interrelated (Rahman and Jackson 2010), but because they help illustrate the dynamic of human rights negotiations since, through gender and sexuality, we see where the challenges and potentialities exist. Also, our conclusion to this chapter brings gender and sexuality back together as analytical constructs. In this chapter, we do not intend to reduce or essentialize gender to women, and sexuality to sexual minorities, even though this reduction is often how it is operationalized by governments, international, and other transnational organizations.

We speak to gendering practices and sexualization beyond behavior and identity.

To be clear, we are not condoning prejudicial treatment against LGBT people and women when we question the deployment of discourses that frame the immigrant subject as essentially needing liberation from oppressive systems. What we are critiquing is the almost automatic hierarchical/racialized/colonial reading embedded in such an understanding of the world. We start with an acknowledgment of the history of colonial relations, and the racial readings that emerge from such historical formations, to discuss racial systems and racialization. This reading of racialization as not only something that happened in the past but as a set of social relations that continue in the present is an important way to apply racialization as a dynamic set of processes. Such conceptualization has the potential to magnify the inherently racialized debates about colonized countries in the pursuit of differentiating themselves from their (former) colonizers, specifically in terms of their treatment of citizens and LGBT citizens.

Following Kibria, Bowman, and O'Leary (2014), we draw on "race as a political project rooted in histories of western colonialism and imperialism" (p. 3) to produce, in this chapter, co-constitutive constructions of modern/savage binaries between the Global North and the Global South.

Our contributions to this chapter are twofold: we show how these discourses construct western countries as more "progressive" on issues around gender and sexuality, while casting the Global South as "backward" (as noted in previous chapters, the West and Global North/South dichotomy is imprecise but still useful to illustrate global power dynamics). These discourses produce particular outcomes: they mask the human rights abuses happening in western countries, and erase the colonial histories and legacies that have altered ways of thinking about race, gender, and sexuality in formerly colonized countries. Secondly, we illustrate how transnational human rights discourses around race, gender, and sexuality are part of a neo-imperial project to try to maintain the presupposed moral superiority of western countries and to demonize the Global South. We discuss a range of issues in international human rights as we insert a racial-colonial reading of the seemingly innocent (and racially colorblind) human rights deployment that oftentimes renders Global South countries and their cultures as underdeveloped. We use cases of gender oppression and sexual minority rights to illustrate racial readings in a transnational and global context. This chapter will tackle specificities of race, gender, and sexuality across a variety of topics and countries. In doing so, the chapter shows how human rights are not only an important globalized construct, but also that they are racialized in the application of the advocacy for gender and sexuality human rights.

The chapter is divided into six sections. We open by defining key terms in order to situate the discussion, and we illustrate the range of human rights mechanisms (as developed in the last century) at the international level; we do so while providing examples of the ways in which gender and sexuality are racialized in the context of various segments of global populations. We then explore how non-governmental organizations (NGOs) are complicit in similar projects and tactics outlined above. We move to historical examples to further contextualize our arguments. Next, we center Jasbir Puar's work and her concept of homonationalism to examine the role of the "proper gay subject" and the "proper" gay citizen's link to nationality. In exploring the connection between international human rights discourses and homonormativity, we will examine how these discourses and political strategies circulate in various countries. Following suit, we include a discussion of a Global North country's efforts to provide equity to migrant Muslim women to elucidate how the state often relies on the homogenization of racialized and gendered groups within political strategizing; we also explore how discourses around same-sex marriage materialize in particular countries in the Global South. We conclude by looking at social movements and other strategies to challenge these neo-imperial projects in the current framing of transnational human rights. In offering other perspectives outside of the traditional areas of study (the international development model), we reveal how race, gender, and sexuality are intimately bound up with transnational human rights, in hopes of proffering ways to challenge their deployments.

Important concepts and context: Why transnational human rights?

The term "human rights" refers to the belief that all human beings have certain inalienable rights. These inalienable rights are understood as universal truths rooted in justice and equality. The Universal Declaration of Human Rights (1948), which was passed by the United Nations General Assembly after World War II, is the main document in which the concept of human rights became fully developed. This document states that there are certain rights that all human beings – regardless of race, sex, nationality, religion, and other protected classes – are inherently entitled to, including "the right to life, liberty, and security of person." Transnational in scope, the Universal Declaration of Human Rights was later foundational to the International Bill of Human Rights. This International Bill of Human Rights became the main international law to monitor human rights and their abuses across countries. In turn, human rights have become a marker by which to measure how much a country has "progressed" in its development within modernity (Stychin 2004).

Human rights expanded to include sexual orientation and gender identity when a group of activists, intellectuals, and policy makers met in November 2006 to draft an international law that would protect sexual and gender minorities from human rights abuses (Thoreson 2009). The final document they produced became known as the Yogyakarta Principles and established "a set of principles on the application of international human rights law in relation to sexual orientation and gender identity" (International Commission of Jurists 2007). These 29 principles were codified in order to challenge and hold accountable laws and practices around the globe that violated the human rights of sexual and gender minorities. They challenged sodomy laws, death penalty laws, and the practice of raping lesbians as a way to "cure" them (Brown 2010). The Yogyakarta Principles conceptualize sexual orientation and gender identity through an identity-based lens, which causes them ultimately to fall short when applied outside of the United States and other western contexts. An identity-based framework fails to capture how laws often focus on criminalizing behavior over identity[1] and also neglects the fact that western identities of sexuality and gender may not be applicable in other countries (Waites 2009). In this way, western countries get to define what constitutes "progress" around sexual orientation and gender identity. Transnational mechanisms, advocacy, and legal recourse are all elements that oftentimes make human rights all over the world inherently a facsimile of those developed in western regions/countries. These discourses are often subtle in how they operate, yet crushing in their expectation that they become homogenized in many parts of the world.

A case in point is the highly reputable Amnesty International USA organization. Their webpage discussion of the human rights of LGBT people emphasizes the need to decriminalize same-sex sexual activities and to pay attention to torture, unemployment, and discrimination, and harassment and verbal abuse. Yet the discussion almost automatically turns to same-sex marriage – a practice that, while valid in its aspiration of securing equal human rights, glosses over all the other elements of discrimination mentioned before. (It also ignores the structural differences in treatment faced by lesbian women, gay men, bisexual people, and trans-identified people – a topic we addressed in the introduction.)

We define "transnational" as that which happens across national borders, issues (economics, politics, social, and structural matters) that impact migrants on both sides of borders/in different countries, and, as others have noted, transnational ties themselves (Faist, Fauser, and Reisenaner 2013). Transnational differs from international in that the "international" scope consists of actions that are carried out by the state and national governments, and uses as units of analyses those given countries (as either "sending" or "host" countries). Given increasing globalization, the role of the state has progressively diminished as external forces, such as multinational corporations and NGOs, influence countries and their decision making (Skogly and Gibney 2002). Transnational is not static but is constantly shifting as power circulates around the world. As the beliefs and traditions of socially dominant actors and forces permeate countries and territories, the fluidity of national boundaries becomes ever apparent, making necessary that the consequences of such a process become identified and negotiated with (Peterson 1992). For example, transnational advocacy networks can hold accountable those nations and governments that claim to be in favor of human rights, and these networks can leverage policy makers to change laws in their respective countries (Keck and Sikkink 1999). Therefore we define "transnational human rights" as the way in which a variety of social actors and forces can globally influence the discourses and implementation of human rights.

Transnational human rights have led to the debate about universalism versus cultural relativism. Who gets to define these "universal truths" about human beings? And how can one understand human rights within specific cultural contexts? A main critique that cultural relativists (people who consider that beliefs and behaviors should be understood within specific cultural contexts) have of universal human rights is that western countries are privileged in defining what counts as a human right and what qualifies as a human rights abuse (Brems 1997). Through economic sanctions, the West can also unilaterally enforce its views of human rights without having to take into account the potential cultural contexts that may shape beliefs about human rights in other (namely, developing) countries (Wall 1998). The construction of universal human rights and their enforcement through economic sanctions imposed by the West has unabridged power in shaping the moral and cultural contexts that impact perspectives of justice and equality. Also, as in the case of several countries in Latin America (see the section in this chapter on Colombia as a Global South comparison), a chain reaction is begun where semi-peripheral countries strike a balance between granting rights to sexual minorities – often reduced to gay, lesbian, bisexual, transgender (LGBT) and intersex (LGBTI)[2] citizens – to gain access to, or remain, "modern" states in the eyes of a global, constantly changing landscape of human rights.

The West – and the rest? How racialized categories of sexuality juxtapose normative ones

As noted in this chapter's opening paragraph, according to the standards set by the United States and other western countries, a minority status based on sexual orientation and/or gender identity carries with it a perceived, real, or symbolic fear of persecution, violence, or death. Migration – whether forced, as in the case of asylum seekers, refugees, and displaced peoples, or voluntary – is often understood to be purely for economic reasons and not due to gender and/or sexual oppression. Nevertheless, migrating people utilize all conduits available to them to improve their lives; however, they may understand these conduits and categories from the perspective of their countries of origin, without necessarily recognizing the full context of the experience in their new countries of residence. As empirical work continues to disrupt the common social perception of gayness as white (Berube 2001; Hunter 2010), other problems arise. In the case of Mexican immigrant men who have sex with men, Cantú (2009) found that the perception of the United States as a gay haven for Mexican immigrant men of lower socioeconomic status was offset by the realities of racism once they arrived in the United States. Moreover, the racist perception of them (and sexual exoticization and racialization) as more sexually adventurous men came particularly from white gay male neighborhoods and communities. As illustrated by Peña (2013) in her work on Cuban *marielitos* (those who arrived in Miami circa 1980), the racialized readings of Cuban queens' effeminate gender expression clashed with the modern (buffed and muscle men) homonormative white gay male. These juxtapositions cannot exist without each other – when the masculine exists, it does so with reference to its negation. Similarly, racial readings of Otherness are exclusionary in specific sexual contexts, as noted by a number of scholars (e.g., Decena 2011; Guzmán 2006). Thus, while newer studies may describe the racialized experiences of other sexual minorities (mostly men – for an exception, see Acosta 2013), such work may inadvertently contribute to a wider perception of a progressive western sexuality vis-à-vis a deficit-based sexual oppression in the rest of the world. The United States is a prime site for this construction, and asylum cases produce many of these narratives (Llewellyn 2015).

In this political maneuver of progressive versus backward countries, the West is able to establish itself as the savior (both of gender and sexuality) whose duty it is to rescue certain "victims" in the Global South from the "savages" in their own country (Mutua 2001), or, as Spivak (1988: 93) states, the "white men are saving the brown women from brown men." An example of this drive to save is the West's construction of female genital surgery (FGS) – often reduced to female genital mutilation (FGM) – as a human rights abuse that they must prevent women in certain countries in the Global South from having to endure (Lewis 1995; Mutua 2001). While the issue of FGS is laden with questions of power, agency, and victimization, Roseanne Njiru and Bandana Purkayastha (2015) offer an analysis of FGS relative to women in Kenya suggesting that the voices of women who have actually experienced FGS/FGM are often erased from the discourse about this practice, as the West, including western feminists, has already constructed FGS as a human rights abuse, thereby eliminating the very possibility that participating in FGS could be an active choice on behalf of some of the research study participants (Njiru and Purkayastha 2015; see also Lewis 1995).[3]

The rhetoric around usage of the hijab and the burka worn by many Muslim women is another telling example.[4] From the onset of US military intervention in Afghanistan, Afghan women were portrayed as needing salvation and liberation from what was seen as a repressive, religious dress code that required them to cover their bodies with conservative attire, sometimes a burka, but most often a hijab. Afghan women became erased as agentic subjects in this process (Ayotte and Husain 2005). The labeling of the hijab as a tool of oppression by white, western feminists casts women living in Muslim-dominant countries as a homogeneous victim group – glossing over the cultural and religious practices of more than a dozen countries and creating a stereotypical misogynist reading of the Muslim faith. This rhetoric also erases the historical use of the veil among middle-class and working-class Iranian women to build coalitional politics, showcasing how the veil is neither inherently oppressive nor religious but may be used for political purposes (Mohanty 1988). This discursive or epistemic violence (enacted by policy makers/government officials, western media, and the masses, and also academics) does not allow the subaltern to speak and is accomplished through this "savages-victims-saviors" human rights discourse and by dehumanizing people in the Global South (Spivak 1988; Mutua 2001; Ayotte and Husain 2005). (We will examine the debate around the use of the hijab more closely in the upcoming comparative case section, which focuses on the mobilization against the alleged practice of Sharia law in Canada in 2003.)

The discourse that paints the West as more progressive and as the savior of those countries that are constructed as backward also masks colonial histories and legacies. In the fall of 2009, certain Ugandan parliamentarians proposed the Anti-Homosexuality Bill, whereby a person in Uganda could be put to death for "aggravated homosexuality" (Cheney 2012). Dubbed the "gay death penalty" bill, many western countries expressed deep concern about the bill, with Sweden threatening to pull all funding from Uganda (Cheney 2012). The debate about this bill, which constructed Uganda as being backward with regard to same-gender desires and practices, completely ignored the colonial history of Uganda and the fact that religious leaders in the United States were behind the bill. This history includes the colonizers' missionary goal of penalizing and eradicating "sexual diversity" (Cheney 2012). This colonial legacy is reminiscent of British rulers in India passing sodomy laws which were also about suppressing same-gender eroticism and practices (Puri 2012). The fact that many of these anti-same-gender laws were passed during colonial rule highlights how many of the views in the postcolonial Global South countries were introduced there by and through the West and its colonial project.[5] In this sense, the colonial legacies and responsibilities of western countries for introducing certain laws now seen as regressive are completely effaced in current transnational human rights discourses about the Global South. Moreover, we may fail to see how a cultural reading of difference (whether based on tribe, religion, "culture," or some other variable) that is produced by *both* the West and the rest results in "the perfect storm" type of scenario.

These oppositional views of culture are enacted for women's bodies and sense of agency as they are for LGBT people. The language of sexual rights, which is meant to be all-encompassing, often references either sexual minority rights or reproductive rights. That is the topic of the next section.

How sexual rights have been internationalized

The language of sexual rights – in human rights applied to gender identity and sexual orientation – is fairly new (Petchesky 2000). It is neither uniformly used nor all-encompassing, in that some countries may reference only LGBT groups while others link it to women's reproductive rights. While scholars discuss the impact of LGBT human rights globally, they also caution that the use of human rights "as a central vehicle and framing device for LGBT political claims" (Kollman and Waites 2009: 2) can be homogenized without regard for local or regional specificities. At the present time, the language (and the phrasing) of human rights (which already presumes sexual rights within it) is the key term in a lot of the international advocacy for LGBT groups and individuals marginalized because of their gender identity and/or sexual orientation.

There are international organizations, such as the International Gay and Lesbian Human Rights Commission (as of late 2015 renamed OutRight Action International) and the International Lesbian and Gay Association (ILGA), that are watchdog groups engaged in moving to an international platform of human rights for LGBT people. Of course, Amnesty International and other bodies that are not LGBT-specific (although, as noted before, they do have LGBT programs within their organizations) offer significant support to these LGBT organizations. These organizations have taken on many fights to make the European Union and United Nations address human rights on the basis of sexual orientation and gender identity.

While these organizations may provide a necessary push to expose discrimination against and hatred of certain groups of people, we would venture to say that the representation and discourses produced in the development of such advocacy merit increased attention (for example, see Wright 2005 for Bolivia's case study). Succinctly, the equation developed among these international watchdog organizations, local activists, the legal enterprise, the local nation-state governances, and cultural practices results in a discourse of progressive/backward analyses. This dichotomy creates a developed western center and a regressive, most often African and Eastern Europe/Middle Easterner, homophobic and repressive outsider system, with East Asia and Latin America represented as more progressive regions – still not as "advanced" as the West, but "getting there."

The processes through which the United States (and some European countries) affirm their position as more democratic is evidenced in the notion of "risk" experienced by asylum seekers in their countries of origin. Claiming a "well-founded fear of prosecution" based on sexual orientation and gender identity, US asylum cases in particular are indicative of this trend. The narrowness with which the state imagines Mexico and other Latin American countries vis-à-vis a welcoming and benevolent US nation is evidenced in these cases (see Cantú 2005; also Cantú 2009). Most often, asylum seekers must establish the reasons why they cannot return to their countries of origin, and those reasons must evidence enough "risk" to justify their fearing for their safety or lives. This framing is a pre-packaged type of narrative that has already been successful in previous legal cases, and the victim narrative is reenacted in order to achieve asylum. Such narratives, along with affidavits from experts (often US/European faculty members and researchers who are experts on that country/region), serve as the basis for the request. While this process is based on a precedent of successful cases in the United States, and thus is logical to lawyers, it reproduces a damaging cultural oppositional reading of asylum seekers' countries of origin. This point is beginning to be articulated in scholarship on asylum-based cases in the United States (see Llewellyn 2015).

What is key to these global negotiations of human rights and sexual rights is that, when it comes from the top down (e.g., from international NGOs), sexual and reproductive rights in different countries do not all work in the same way, nor do they deploy the same type of authority, with LGBT (often just gay and lesbian) rights ahead of any women's rights. We now explore the colonial and postcolonial impacts of these laws and discourses in Puerto Rico and India to further our argument about how certain transnational human rights become hegemonic.

Well-intentioned hegemonies

Human rights discourses are expressed as being universally relevant and applicable to individuals, whatever the localities or experiences of individuals. As noted previously, human rights are coded, oftentimes to reflect development goals associated with providing human security for individuals (generally sexual minorities and women) in developing nations. The initiatives implemented on behalf of human rights and development reflect singular constructions of the "third world woman" and assume a one-size-fits-all strategy to overcome a multitude of discrete obstacles (Eisenstein 2009). Human rights are directed by western notions of modernity; modernizing, in and of itself, is defined by and embedded in what can be purchased or consumed. By focusing on consumption, neoliberal pushes for modernity have opted to provide women with jobs in a process of global industrialization. Instead of empowering women, such initiatives risk women being further exploited through labor for the benefit of multinational corporations. Instead of zeroing in on human rights discourse and employing what Eisenstein refers to as "hegemonic feminism," scholars have utilized human security as an arguably better framework, centering the voices and needs of the individuals that human rights often overlook. A human security framework is deliberate in its understanding that exploitation and insecurity occur differently, depending on the locality they occur within. By rejecting a human rights discourse, which achieves its functionality by superimposing a sameness on the two-thirds world,[6] gender and sexuality become nuanced, and movements toward achieving equality have less chance of becoming stagnated by oversimplification. This oversimplifying of the two-thirds world and the social, political, and economic matters it experiences are articulated through the bodies of women. During historical moments of political upheaval, specific expressions of sexuality have become deviant and framed as necessitating intervention. Iterations of this phenomenon are rooted in the formation of a racialized, sexualized "other" in an effort to delineate members of the elite ranks of society. One such case study involves the policing of sexuality in Puerto Rico during the late eighteenth century.

Utilizing sexuality as a means to culturalize and racialize behavior is by no means a new practice. The following discussion links Puerto Rico and India in a comparative case study to show how sexuality has been shaped by hierarchical colonial power structures in both countries. These power structures derive from the colonial occupation both localities experienced and are thus inherently racialized.[7] The colonial legacy present in both Puerto Rico and India instilled specific machineries that marked individuals as different through racialization. These racialized, colonial hierarchies became articulated through sexuality and the body. In the case of Puerto Rico's transition from Spanish colonialism to US domination in the late 1800s through the early 1920s, the social demarcation of "honor" was constructed in approximation to exhibiting qualities coded through whiteness (Findlay 1999). Whiteness, in this instance, becomes defined not only as an indication of light skin, but also as a heightened social class in which members practiced sexuality through socially bound means, in which light skin together with sexual piety gave certain families social privilege. Light-skinned, high-class women (who would be considered white in the United States) in Puerto Rico during this time occupied a privileged sphere in society that allowed their sexual practices to be understood as ideal and respectable. Individual respectability was measured and defined through one's ability to perform whiteness through sexuality. Decency as both a racialized and classed construct drew distinct boundaries between elites and plebeians, a distinction rooted in presumed sexual difference between black and white Puerto Ricans.

Methods of population control impacted Puerto Rico during the 1970s. Efforts by the state to sterilize women took on contested meaning during this time. Sterilization used means that deliberately annulled women's agency and was at times decided upon by a male figure, most commonly a woman's spouse. Contestations of sterilization see it as a state-driven tool used to actively reduce the number of poor women giving birth in Puerto Rico and frame it as a means of practicing agency over the body. According to this school of thought, women exhibited the agency to decide to become sterilized as a means of birth control. In this interpretation, it is important to critically analyze the assumptions about poor women and their governance over their bodies. How do truths around body sovereignty become nuanced in the case of low-income women? What assumptions do these truths rely on, not only in terms of racialization, but of income level and education as well?

Morality's conflation with racialized representations of sexuality codes non-white individuals as hypersexual and sexually aggressive. Specifically, prostitution in Ponce during the late 1870s came under attack as cleansing efforts swept through the city. Largely backed by upper-class communities, these efforts racialized sexual behaviors as dichotomous: black as immoral and white as chaste. The centering of sexuality as a means of defining moral forms of being is interweaved with the sociopolitical project of creating proper female subjects who contribute to the *gran familia* (the big, united family narrative). The impetus on constructing a "decent" female subject became so materialized that elite Puerto Rican men also participated in this practice by defining proper womanhood through motherhood and purity. The bodies of Puerto Rican women became physical and symbolic manifestations of racial and gendered differences that acted as a metaphor for the political tensions on the island.

Outside the context of Puerto Rico and other geographic regions where a black/white binary is applicable, racialization does not lend itself usefully as a tool for noting how sexuality is constructed through larger, organizing frameworks in localities such as India. The theoretical frameworks of racial formations and intersectionality do not have the same meanings in such a locality, where other salient social organizers, such as caste, shape essentialized understandings of race and necessitate a framework that moves beyond race-based groupings. Jyoti Puri (2012) illustrates the power of homophobic legislative efforts in the context of India, where a moral imperative to criminalize homosexuality has instigated exceptionally violent activities. The state, Puri argues, is messy and disconnected, and so are the ways in which regulation happens – these are not coordinated well. By linking state-led sterilization in Puerto Rico and the criminalization of sodomy in India, it becomes evident that a dominant group's command of sexuality is not only consequential in terms of how certain constructions of acceptable sexuality become internalized but, perhaps more importantly, in how these dominant constructions can lead to state-sanctioned violence.

Sodomy laws have been cited as a justification for imposing violent action on non-heterosexual subjects suspected of violation. Penal codes that criminalize homosexual acts concede enforcement rights to general public bodies, which have used these codes to commit heinous homophobic acts. By way of institutionalizing a ban on certain sexualities through the state, the latter inadvertently grants citizens the implicit right to enforce homophobic laws. This implicit rendering of citizens as guardians of the state has pushed non-heterosexual subjects further into the margins, making them vulnerable to various forms of aggression. It also further stigmatizes individuals who are HIV-positive or have AIDS due to erroneous assumptions about what kinds of individuals tend to be infected. Media attention as well as public demonstrations opposing Code 377 – the "unnatural offense" law in India that included same-sex sexual activities – resulted in its reform. This reformation carved a space for sexual citizenship in India.

In both colonial/postcolonial situations discussed, the exercise of power through a hegemonic lens is evidenced. The people internalize the "ideal-type" systems of the ruling class (in this case, a colonial order) that has clearly demarcated views on racial hierarchies and their value or lack thereof. There is significant involvement of the state in regulating that almost naturalized view – either by reinforcing it peacefully or by controlling those who resist. These normalizing forces not only operate in the context of gender, race, and class – they also do so in terms of sexuality, often with globalizing implications that value/devalue according to hegemonic standards.

On homonationalism (and the racialized markings by first-world gay people)

In this section, we turn to Jasbir Puar's concept of homonationalism in order to elucidate the ways in which notions of sexual rights are utilized with race-specific implications. In particular, we examine how discourses around certain gay rights are called upon to justify the war on terror and to further Islamophobia. We first lay out Puar's concept of homonationalism. From there, we turn to the Dutch case in order to examine how Puar's concept is used not just to justify the war on terror but also to discipline Muslim immigrants in the Netherlands. We also look at the case of "pinkwashing" in Israel to discuss how gay rights in Israel are used to demonize Palestine and to vindicate the occupation of Palestinian land. In the end, we find homonationalism to be a useful analytical framework to illuminate how gender and sexual transnational human rights discourses are inherently bound up with notions of race and the racializing of western and Middle Eastern states and bodies.

In *Terrorist Assemblages*, Jasbir Puar (2007) coins the term "homonationalism" to show how the justification for war and other interventions in the Middle East include United States military personnel adopting discourses about liberating gay and lesbian people in the Middle East, while simultaneously using gay epithets such as "fag" to demonize Muslims. Homonationalism is the melding of Duggan's (2002) concept of homonormativity with nationalism. Homonormativity is a political strategy used within sexual minority communities that reinforces heteronormative institutions and mores (Duggan 2002). Sexual minorities seek these rights through consumption practices, monogamy, marriage, domesticity, and reproduction. Homonationalism, then, is the folding of certain homonormative gay and lesbian subjects into the life of the nation, while demonizing Muslims for being "backward" on gay and lesbian issues and subjugating Muslim people, specifically through torture, detention, and murder. A country being gay-friendly is a marker of being "modern, cosmopolitan, developed, first-world, [G]lobal [N]orth, and most significantly, democratic" (Puar 2011: 138). In this regard, the barometer measuring a country's treatment of women, used in colonial times to justify colonization, has become one gauging how it treats gay and lesbian people, which is now used to justify invasions and the war on terror (Puar 2011).

Puar argues that homonationalism is the configuration of three practices: sexual exceptionalism, regulatory queerness, and the ascendancy of whiteness. Sexual exceptionalism is evident in western nations (for Puar, mainly the United States), claiming par excellence on LGBT issues and demonizing Muslim countries for lagging behind in this area. This sexual exceptionalism is used as a "missionary discourse" to justify the invasions of Afghanistan and Iraq as a supposed strategy to save sexual minorities in these countries. It is also a queer regulatory device, in that queer Muslims are seen as not having agency and being in need of saving. The "proper" homosexual subject is seen as white, and western nations can implement homophobic practices and discourses to discipline certain racialized subjects, while still claiming to be progressive around issues of sexuality and gender. Homonationalist discourses also gloss over the failed achievement of equality for LGBT people in certain western countries where, for instance, they experience employment and housing discrimination. Countries in the Global South are presented as homogenized, even though certain countries in the Global South have been leaders in addressing certain human rights abuses and at the forefront of sexual and gender equality. Ultimately, for Puar (2013: 337), homonationalism is the "historical convergence of state practices, transnational circuits of queer commodity culture and human rights paradigms, and broader global phenomena such as the increasing entrenchment of Islamophobia."

Within this historical convergence, a terrorist masculinity becomes imagined, whereby Muslim bodies are seen as failed and perverse. Terrorists are constructed and regulated through the lens of monstrosity and a failed heterosexuality;

their sexuality is seen as excessive (Puar and Rai 2002). This construction of the terrorist works as a disciplinary device to instruct people in the United States how to be a patriot – how to be properly heterosexual or gay. It also depicts a monolithic Muslim culture and dehumanizes Muslim people. This dehumanization allows for the torture of Muslim detainees, whereby practices of sodomy are used against them as a weapon of war. As a means to emasculate the terrorists (for emasculating the United States on 9/11), they are constructed as "fags." This weapon is considered effective since Muslim people are constructed as homophobic; therefore, the threat of sodomy and being labeled and called a "fag" are imagined as being the worst forms of torture and verbal abuse to be inflicted upon Muslim bodies. This construction of the terrorist, though, is via the representation of the West as having "respectable" gay and lesbian subjects, whose sexuality is seen as proper and not excessive (Amar 2011; for LGBT respectability politics, see Ward 2007).

Outside of the war on terror, homonationalism also works to justify Islamophobia in the building of certain nation-states, especially in the framing of immigration as a threat to certain western nations (El-Tayeb 2012). In the Netherlands, some Dutch officials paint Holland as the main site of gender and sexual liberation. In constructing themselves as this paradigm, certain Dutch citizens cast Muslim culture and religion as backward and immigrant Muslims as people who need to assimilate properly into "liberal" Dutch society (Bracke 2012). Gender and sexual liberation actually become part and parcel of who belongs to the Dutch nation and who does not (Bracke 2012). In this regard, accepting gay men and sexual liberation becomes the hallmark of citizenship in neoliberal modernity (Mepschen, Duyvendark, and Tonkens 2010). The new trope of "white men saving brown women from brown men" now becomes "white men saving white gay men from brown men" (Bracke 2012). This trope is basically white heterosexual men saving white gay men from "backward" brown men and immigrants.

For example, for the civic integration test, immigrants are taught about gay people and are instructed to tolerate homosexuality if they want to live in the Netherlands (Bracke 2012). Tolerance becomes part of being "civilized" (Denike 2010), and homophobia becomes constructed as only existing in ethnic and religious communities and not as part of the broader Dutch culture. Likewise, the Dutch homo-emancipation policy frames the social acceptance of Dutch gay people through an identity-based "out" lens (Jivraj and de Jong 2011). This document also paints Muslim communities as the core target group that needs to learn this social acceptance. As in Britain, Muslim and homophobia become conflated (Haritaworn, Tauqir, and Erdem 2008). It also inscribes a "speakability" imperative, whereby the homonormative citizenship model is to be "out" and visibly queer (Jivraj and de Jong 2011). It does not allow for other ways of being queer outside of this western "coming out" framework.

The debate around Islam and homophobia also completely erases queer Muslims (El-Tayeb 2012). Seen as too oppressed to speak for themselves, queer Muslims can only take on a western gay identity through assimilating into western culture (El-Tayeb 2012). Muslim women, gay men, and lesbians are seen as victims of their culture who must adopt Dutch ways in order to find true liberation. Only queer Muslims who do assimilate are granted a voice, and they are seen as the exception to demonstrate how backward other Muslim people are (Bracke 2012; El-Tayeb 2012). This "human rights industrial complex" and its discourses around gay and lesbian identities privileges "coming out" and identity politics as the "proper" and dominant way of being a homonormative subject (Puar 2013). As Fatima El-Tayeb (2012: 80) states, "It is only when they can make the step into western modernity – a step that necessarily requires the break with, the coming out of the Muslim community – that they can claim an individualized identity as feminist or queer, usually by expressing gratitude for being saved by their 'host society.'" This form of sexual citizenship does not take into account cultural diversity, and it privileges western-based notions of sexual identity and subjecthood (Mepschen, Duyvendark, and Tonkens 2010).

Homonationalism also operates in Israel as well to construct Israel as modern and Palestine as barbaric (Puar 2011). Certain activists have coined this strategy as "pinkwashing," whereby Israel markets itself as queer-friendly and as a global gay vacation destination, while concealing the human rights abuses that are inflicted on Palestinians (Schulman 2011). The public relations campaign "Brand Israel" was used to depict Israel as relevant and modern, while painting Palestine as homophobic. Again, this strategy also completely erases queer Palestinians or the gay rights organizations that exist in Palestine. Israel, like the United States and the Netherlands, becomes seen as liberal, progressive, and civilized, erasing the homophobic oppression that actually occurs in Israel (Puar 2011). The occupation of Palestine, and how it affects the cultural norms and values of Palestine, is also erased (Puar 2011).

In this section, we have shown how the rise of particular gay rights discourses in certain western nations is part and parcel of the rise of Islamophobia. Homonationalism is the analytical framework coined to explain this phenomenon, in that in this historical moment we must be critical of accepting some gay subjects into the nation-state at the expense of Muslim bodies. As the Dutch and Israeli cases reveal, homonationalism works not only to justify the war on terror, but also to discipline Muslim immigrants and to efface human rights abuses in one's own country. These transnational human rights discourses around sexuality and gender clearly operate in race-specific ways that demonize bodies of color, allowing for the proliferation of violence on particular brown and black bodies. Ultimately, new ways of thinking about sexual citizenship that take into account cultural and religious diversity are needed in order to challenge the hegemonic western notions of LGBT human rights currently in operation. In thinking through these concepts and issues, we now provide a northern comparative case, followed by a Global South case.

A northern comparative case

There exists an assumed lack of female agency, particularly in women from the Global South, which is communicated through the racialization of identities related to certain religions and nationalities. Despite the fact that it is practiced in many parts of the world in diverse ways, Islam experiences homogenization and becomes racialized, ultimately marking Muslim people as "other," brown, and dangerous. This rendition causes Muslim women to be understood as existing under a constant threat of a "radical" Islam, whose practices are seen as existing in opposition to western feminism (see Lâm 1994). What happens in the process is the aforementioned savage-victim-savior paradigm, which has become especially evident in ongoing debates over use of the hijab and the burka, as well as within public misconceptions and fear of Sharia law.

The ability of Muslim women in Canada to act in their own self-interest was called into question in 2003 when legislators in Ontario, Canada, mobilized against what was understood to be the practice of Sharia law within the arbitration services provided by the Islamic Institute of Civil Justice (Korteweg 2008). The services became available to consenting participants and took into account local laws in an effort to find equitable, religiously based solutions to clients' issues, either within families or in businesses. After controversy ensued over the institute's arbitration practice in 2006, the Ontario Arbitration Act was passed, and all forms of religious intervention in matters of business and family disputes became outlawed (regardless of the religion).

The way in which the matter of religious arbitration was portrayed and subsequently handled by the media relied on essentialized, reductionist interpretations of Muslim women's positionality and their alleged lack of choice and agency. In this process, Muslim identification was saturated with erroneous assumptions around extremism and radicalism that had first been associated with Islam following

September 11. These beliefs formed the foundation for the "othering" of Muslim women and located them socially as passive receivers of patriarchal oppression, namely by way of religious imperatives that instituted male dominance. It also accounted for a singular framing of Sharia law, which became dubbed as inherently oppressive toward women. Sharia law contains a range of interpretations from highly conservative underpinnings to far more liberal understandings; the reductionist "ethnicizing" of Islam by way of attributing acts such as honor killings to Muslim faith fomented the savage-victim-savior paradigm on behalf of white feminists in Canada.

Beyond the "othering" property of the Ontario Arbitration Act, this piece of legislation, enacted by the state, essentially enforced a dichotomous expression of Muslim women's agency: one could either reject Islam and be empowered, or be devout and backward in terms of women's rights (Korteweg 2008). By not recognizing the potential for Muslim women to be both devout and empowered, the state rejected what has been coined "embedded agency," which recognizes that the resistance of any entire institution (e.g., religion) relies on a homogenized representation of that institution and asserts that one can exercise agency within religious contexts and practices. This process of homogenization led to a particular racialization in the case of Islam in Ontario, whereby Islam was primarily practiced by immigrants. In addition to the racialized nature of immigrant status, Muslims became marked by brownness and their assumed radicalness, while any subscription to Islam became automatically read as existing in opposition to gender equality. The opposition to religious arbitration in Ontario was based on an outright rejection of the idea that a woman in a religious context could exercise power and control, regardless of her own interpretation of her participation within it. Another set of contradictions in the evolution of this transnational human rights approach is embodied in same-sex rights – the topic of our next case comparison.

A Global South comparative case

In this section, we address the case of Colombia's same-sex legal unions. After Uruguay, Brazil, Mexico, and Argentina, other countries – including Costa Rica, Chile, Colombia, and Ecuador – approved a marital-like (or de facto) union between same-sex partners. Some of these countries have taken a seemingly "cut and paste" approach, transplanting transnational human rights into their country. This section will detail the potentiality of a kind of "mimicry" of north-ern human rights to show the extent to which those travel and are successful in those other sites.

Colombia has several regions, and Bogotá, the capital, is at the forefront of establishing public policies to recognize same-sex relationships. Bogotá is a city with an amalgam of ideas and projects and policies, oftentimes developed else-where and fused with its own ideas and culture and religious restrictions. These interconnections can be seen in the agenda-setting power of US activists, the deployment of such agendas, and the changes and incorporation of these agendas in different places. In the end, hegemonic, hetero- and homonormative elements remain in the agendas of activists and academics, and permeate into the negotiations with lawmakers in fighting for same-sex rights. A changing land-scape of sexual politics (in the United States and Europe) has clear impact in terms of the politically efficacious changes elsewhere – for instance, the notion of gay marriage is a notion that has traveled so much globally, whereas other challenges to human rights not so much: the rights for tran-sitioning for transgender people, or the need to focus our attention on the inequalities within LGBT communities in terms of class, race, ability, or age (the latter discussions we have seen in the United States more recently). While not intending to say that these political battles should not impact agendas elsewhere, we seek to advocate that we move beyond an ethnocentric approach that suggests any proposed politi-cal change in the North/West will be equally productive elsewhere. Activists and academics willing to critique mainstream approaches do so within the US/European context, yet sometimes fail to see that the items that do make it to a national agenda, even if they are later dropped, in fact cross borders quite easily, thanks to international networks and NGOs, as well as to the internet. Sometimes the normativity of the project at hand also percolates into other settings. We hope to show this using the Colombian case.

Spotlight 3.1 Contradictions and Advancements in Colombia: Some Context

Advances in Colombia, developed for over two decades now, have established and expanded the rights of LGBT(I) citizens. Starting with the revised constitution of 1991, Colombia offers the right for children born intersex to choose, at a later moment in life, their identification and surgical sex/gender affirmation, if desired; it is still (as of 2017) the only country in the Americas to do so. The government provides funding for and has a policy focus on LGBT rights, and it coordinates objectives between women's services and LGBT organizing. Public policies in Bogotá and, more recently, Medellín and Cali have moved beyond the notion of sexual minorities into a multicultural language of sorts – *diversidad sexual* – that loosely translates as sexual diversity. Since the middle of the last decade, the nomenclature change has attempted to establish LGBT people as prototypical citizens and members of a community. People who feel their rights have been violated can submit a tutelage action (a *tutela*, or tutelage, is a formal/legal complaint, less rigid than a lawsuit but nonetheless an initiating element for investigation and the "right" of a wrong; there are thousands of *tutelas* lodged all over the country every year). These legal actions help address biases against LGBT people. Since the 1991 constitution reinserts every person as a citizen with rights, LGBT people enter the public imaginary, as their "rights," like those of any citizen, are fully incorporated. In that, the "diversity" term has them join Afro-Colombians, indigenous groups, and women as the groups most deeply affected by structural discrimination and lack of resources.

At the same time, Bogotá, and Colombia more generally, offers us a great set of contradictions that are useful when advocating for LGBT rights, even when the risks are great. With a strong Catholic, Opus Dei, and fervent evangelical constituency, LGBT activists' task to change the cultural landscape is an uphill battle. But there are many spaces that have opened up for small cultural changes to take place – in what seem the least likely locations. For instance, the first author – Vidal-Ortiz – was affiliated with a research institute at the Pontificia Universidad Javeriana, a Jesuit institution, where one of the leading researchers is a trans woman, Brigitte Baptiste, who heads the Humboldt Institute and brings international recognition and funding to the Javeriana. Ciclo Rosa (translated as Lavender or Pink Cycle) is a forum where academics, artists, and activists converse and produce work together; this cycle is also sponsored by the university, and there is no other like it in Colombia. There are as many places of encounter for members of the LGBT communities as in any main US city, despite a strong conservative presence among leaders at academic and governmental institutions, not to mention the paramilitaries and the work of "social cleansing" done within Colombia – these guerrillas take the opportunity, whenever possible, to kill LGBT people, people living with HIV, and sex workers (particularly trans women). The latter structural circumstances pressurize and influence migration patterns of LGBT people and create the conditions for internal displacement.

Among these challenges and contradictions, the government in main cities advocates for and establishes services targeting LGBT Colombians. For instance, there are several community centers in the principal gay, LGBT, or trans-specific neighborhoods in Bogotá; the city of

Bogotá hires more than 150 LGBT employees (under different types of employment – some contract, some full-time) to operate under the Bogotá Humana (a more humane Bogotá) program that specifically focuses on LGBT people; there are key gay, lesbian, and trans government employees in various public positions (government jobs). All of these different services, centers, and employment programs make Bogotá a pretty "gay-friendly" place that attempts to offer previously unheard of services; these services, centers, and programs are in some ways due to the influence/pressure of an international and global network.

It is common to see some of the slogans of US advocacy in public relations campaigns for same-sex marriage rights in Colombia, without much attention being paid to the local context. For instance, in the video *10 Reasons Why Equality Marriage is Needed* by Colombia Diversa,[8] some of the reasons given are: we seek a fair and just society; homosexuality is not a mental illness; families in Colombia are so diverse that the nuclear family is in the minority; it is cost-beneficial; and that – and we have to love this one – since animals have same-sex sexual acts, then human sexuality is not based merely on reproductive goals. Yet there is also the discourse of development (and the pressure from international bodies, often cited, as well as the mention of other countries whose agendas have included same-sex marriage); as Colombia is a country with a secular foundation, marriage should be seen as a legal contract, and not a religious affirmation; and lastly, there is the uncritical comparison (that often takes place in the United States and Europe) of the advocacy for same-sex rights with slavery and its abolition. This last strategy carries the most problematic assumptions about human rights and LGBT social movements: unlike in the United States, Colombia's government continuously addresses neglect – both historical and current – to ethno-racial minorities, so the "cut and paste" approach differs in its impact. It also seems highly controversial to conflate a right to life from two centuries ago with the right to reach the equality so few are close to in the twenty-first century. These issues do not translate well in the Colombian context, yet through media and the internet they become part of the banner of equality in a country with a very different history of slavery and exploitation, religiously, economically, and socially.

With the United Nations and other international bodies continuously achieving gains for human rights based on gender identity and sexual orientation, the framing of equality has shifted by adding external pressure to countries which resist offering such rights. For instance, the 2011 resolution – the first ever – on human rights for sexual minorities "request[ed] the High Commissioner for Human Rights to prepare a study on violence and discrimination on the basis of sexual orientation and gender identity, and call[ed] for a panel discussion to be held at the Human Rights Council to discuss the findings of the study in a constructive and transparent manner, and to consider appropriate follow-up."[9] Countries like Colombia, with such a strong public policy platform, hold onto these discussions to establish this agenda as a priority in order to change the public perception of equality and rights for LGBT people. Indeed, in comparison with Colombia, the United States has some learning to do. And yet the beginnings of the advocacy for these human rights for LGBT people – again, often reduced to same-sex marriage – were in countries, like the United States, where same-sex marriage was approved in 2015, years later than other places in Latin America.

A different model?

As noted in the introduction, in this chapter we were interested in addressing the circulation not only of marked bodies (as we did in the previous chapter) but also of processes of stigmatization and the treatment of migrants in this transnational world. We wanted to engage with the way that governments in the Global North and the Global South have reconfigured themselves by supporting a colonial/racial order through sexuality and gender in the name of transnational human rights. We aimed to show that in many places a "ranking" of diversity – in this case, of sexual diversity – carries a great deal of political and economic international recognition. Indeed, African countries fear a loss of funding, whereas Asian and Latin American ones that are seen as progressive are advancing in other globalizing processes. In differentiating these countries as progressive or backward, racialized readings are enacted and solidified. That, to our minds, is an important contribution of the queering of the otherwise homogenizing transnational human rights/sexual rights system we see in place. These hierarchies of progress, or lack thereof, in terms of sexuality have little impact on gender and, more specifically, reproductive rights; for instance, in some Latin American countries that seem to grant same-sex partners a lot of benefits, their local governments continue to impose – and in some cases increase – penalties for abortion (from social stigma and shaming to the reduction of resources, and legal maneuverings to curtail reproductive services/rights). This unevenness of social change and human rights of course necessitates further research, but suffice it to say that a globalized sexual/human rights order hides within a hierarchical value of bodies and the control of reproductive rights, and those are often racialized on the ground: the poor, often indigenous and of African heritage, are the ones facing most of the regulation.

We conclude this chapter by connecting gender and sexuality to social movements in order to challenge what we see as neo-imperial projects of a current framing (what we call transnational human rights) that homogenize all gender and sexuality rights as same-sex marriage rights (disregarding all reproductive rights), while capitalizing on a West/rest binary that demonizes the rest. (We see this homogenizing discourse as the main challenge to how a platform of racialized sexualities and genders get solidified on a global political scale.) As scholars engaged in social movement work, we see sexual and reproductive rights language as productive in regions of the Global South. A case in point is the Andean region of

South America, and Latin America more broadly, which tends to be more coalitional – where women's and gender issues-led government agencies, NGOs, and temporal movements take on the sexual diversity agenda, not to co-opt it but to incorporate it into their work (Vidal-Ortiz, Viteri, and Serrano 2014). Governments that operate with what may seem to some in the North to be disparate agendas (access to reproductive services and abortion, and services to trans women, alongside social services for gay men, for instance) are actually at odds but result in positive outcomes for all those involved. Such coalitional politics is not the case in a lot of western countries: one cannot imagine homonormative white gay men, for instance, serving as escorts to guarantee women access to their local Planned Parenthood clinics, shielding them from the religious righters who try to block their entry, in any US city. Thus the disconnect between the North and the South in terms of women's and LGBT rights makes the challenge much broader in the United States/ Europe than elsewhere, and in some ways, turns (queers) the socio- and geopolitical understanding of progress in the North against the backdrop of the Global South.

A different model would be a project of coalitional engagement, as in feminist politics and social movements. This model would entail a different understanding of the needs of "minorities" inasmuch as gender and sexuality, and their intersecting racializing and colonial constructs, impact whole populations who often fight for their individualized rights (in the first wave of feminism in the United States, black women waited for the recognition of their rights; more recently, we saw how transgender rights were also marginalized within mainstream gay and lesbian organizing with the United States). Such a model is compulsorily intersectional and looks at the multiple variables of social inequalities. With transgender rights being a slow-moving project in western countries, but making progress in parts of the Global South, we see the need for a continuous engagement with these elements beyond a same-sex marriage agenda – indeed, the urgency has never been more evident.

The next chapter, "Racing Sex Work," furthers the analysis provided here by confronting this savior narrative in the realm of erotic labor and its evident racialized component. Like this chapter, chapter 4 complicates immigration and race analyses by moving the discussion to racialization strategies. It expands the discussion by inter-articulating sexual, gendered, and racialized desire in the context of erotic labor, sex work, and prostitution.

4

Racing Sex Work

In this chapter, we turn to the topic of international sex work in order to explore the raced, classed, gendered, and sexualized components of erotic labor and its embodiment. We also provide an analysis of discourses around the enactments of desire. Sex work is often understood as solely related to the fields of gender and sexuality, but we will show the connections with race that are always implicated in discussions about sex work, desire, and erotic labor. This examination, like the previous chapter, continues to build on our understanding of the relationship between migration and race as we move discussions toward racialization. While the previous chapter engaged in questions of race and migration in relation to human rights discourses – where "progressive" countries are shaming those of indigenous, mixed-race, Middle Eastern, and black heritage for being "backward" – this chapter describes the links between migration and racialized readings of desire, and how those categories are mutually constitutive in framing sex work in discursive ways. We will not only explore the experiences of immigrants and non-white sex workers but also how desire is imbricated within whiteness (or its proxy, as noted shortly). Thus this chapter is about the application of different racialization systems – systems intertwined with migration (where migration then becomes an element of racialization) – and how these racialization systems influence popular readings and ideological discourses of sex work and erotic labor.

Through migration, the local and the global together organize, in critical ways, our discussion of sex work, erotic labor, desire, and race. Because we explore these links at an international level, migration and race are intrinsically linked in this chapter as well – as is often the case, immigrants are highly stigmatized yet simultaneously desired (as a forbidden fruit of sorts), and, in terms of sex work and prostitution,[1] are the target of "saviors" and the "rescue industry" (Agustín 2007). These issues are visible in any given country or territory, as racialized practices are foundational in thinking and deploying raced and gendered innocence (such as white slavery discourses) vis-à-vis the dangerous, ill, or contaminated sex worker who is more often than not desired and feared simultaneously, and is often non-white (or at least read as such). Underneath the terrain of desire and Otherness are inherently political economic issues – dire need, financial need, and economic crises, for sure – that in many ways structure how the exotic sex worker Other is read in any given territory, which often leads onlookers to assume an intrinsic relationship between human trafficking, sexual trafficking and exploitation, prostitution, sex work, and the phenomenon of "mail-order brides." As we illustrate in this chapter, those conflations serve globalized projects of continuous exploitation, of "rescue industries" that are inherently xenophobic, and of the regulation of desire through racial homogeneity.

These sexual and racial readings can also be connected to temporary migration, in the form of tourism: while immigration frameworks will elicit a racialized reading of immigrants who are often non-white, sex tourism often implies a classed and raced self-racialization (as non-marked, as white/ European) through traveling, as well as the sexual racialization of Other places – be they the Caribbean (Kempadoo 2004), South Africa (Walker and Oliveira 2015), South Asia

(Chin 2013), or Brazil (da Silva and Blanchette 2009; Williams 2011), to name but a few.[2]

This brief introduction should explain what we aim to show in this chapter: that sex work and erotic labor are always already racialized. What we mean by racialization, in this chapter and throughout this book, is a marking of groups with hierarchical meaning. We refer to the structuring way of systematically controlling and subjugating non-white bodies, and stereotypically desiring and pigeonholing non-white individuals, as a process of racialization. We also intend to illustrate that racialization is enabled through migration and the difference created by racialized readings of host/migrating societies, be it historical – as in US racial formations that created blackness (in and through slavery) as an inferior category – or in the present with the flow of migrants for a range of reasons, what are sometimes called push–pull factors (for the origins of migration theory, see Lee 1966).[3] This migratory focus also represents an inherently comparative racialization argument, in general, and in the context of sex work in particular. We discuss the ways in which racialized bodies are part of a global or a local articulation of desires, and engage with the hypersexualized/ undersexualized readings of bodies of color, which in the United States (and increasingly, a globalized world) often takes place in and through gender – by both hyper-masculinizing darker male and female bodies, and feminizing Asian male bodies. We will also show how racial innocence, which is often racialized as, by, and through whiteness, is used to foreground trafficked people who need saving and, at the same time, to produce an erotic capital for white women that is not always available to women of color, spatially or in the realm of fantasy.[4] Sex workers of color, by contrast, are often seen and perceived as street-based prostitutes who are violating laws, are themselves the cause of urban disorder, and are constantly being criminalized (by unjustified stereotyping). Ultimately, this chapter will explicate how sex work is not just about gender inequality and patriarchy (the usual feminist argument) but is also about nationalism, racism, migration patterns, and colonial legacies linked to sexuality, the erotic, and desire.

This chapter is divided into four sections. We begin by situating terms to better describe for the reader the categories of erotic labor, sex work, and sexual tourism, but we consciously separate them from notions of trafficking or other erotic labor practices in order to outline different lines of inquiry that are often ignored in images of sex work as something that is "forced" and often synonymous with "trafficked." We then complicate the discussion with a review section based on literature adding other categories that bring in racial, migratory, and transnational aspects, starting with women-of-color erotic labor in juxtaposition to white women's erotic and sexual scripts, and then move on to clarifying common conflations of sex work, trafficking, and "mail-order brides." The following section offers two case studies: one on sex work and immigration in relation to "rescue industries"; and another case study on sex tourism. We then conclude with implications for the study of migration and race, gender and sexuality, and erotic labor and sex work.

Context for sex work and related concepts

Sex work is often defined as an occupation where someone is hired to provide sexual services for money (Minichiello, Scott, and Callander 2013). Sex work can range from prostitution and work in pornography to peep shows, lap dancing, webcam sex, and any other service that qualifies as some form of sexual performance for monetary gain (for women's erotic acts in person and on camera, see Chapkis 1997 and Jones 2015; for men, see Seymour 2008). Prostitution, which is often one of the most discussed forms of sex work, is engaging in sexual relations for money (Beran 2012). Prostitution, though, is often illegal because people are seen as being paid for sex, whereas, in the case of pornography, people are seen as being paid to act (Leung 2003). Also, in the United States, for example, pornography is protected under the First Amendment, and since a third party is paying for the service, it is not illegal, whereas prostitution is illegal in most of the country (Calvert and Richardson 2006). To further demonstrate the power of this sex industry, one can look at its revenue. The global porn revenues in 2007 were around US$20 billion, and the previous year the total sex-related entertainment business in the United States made around US$13 billion (Covenant Eyes 2015). Although definitions of sex work and what is legal versus illegal may be slippery at times and vary both within and among countries, it is undeniable that sex work is a profitable global industry.

Within this globalized world, sex tourism allows people to travel to another country with the objective of engaging in sexual activity, often with prostitutes (Kempadoo 1999). Sex tourism is normally thought of as (presumably) heterosexual men from the Global North traveling to countries in the Global South to seek sexual pleasure with women because sexual services are cheaper in these Global South countries than in the North (Oppermann 1999). Studies have documented that people who seek same-sex encounters also participate in sex tourism and travel to other countries for sexual pleasure (Oppermann 1999; Padilla 2007). In fact, as certain Global South countries have shifted to service economies, sex industries and sex tourism have expanded in order to generate sustainable profits for Global South countries (Padilla 2007). However, sex tourism and sex industries are also part of ascending economies, such as that of Vietnam, complicating the monolithic picture that sex tourism is just about powerful people from dominant economies (read: the Global North) traveling to the "developing" Global South and the assumption that people from the Global North are the most elite or desired within these sex industries (Hoang 2015).

Sex trafficking has emerged as a controversial topic that has complicated people's understanding of sex work. Sex trafficking is the trade of humans for the purpose of sexual exploitation (Kara 2010). It entails coercion, forced labor, and sexual slavery (Butcher 2003). "Trafficking is slavery because it includes fraud or extortion in recruitment and coercion, restraint, gang rape, threat of physical harm, loss of liberty, and loss of self-determination on arrival in the destination industry" (Schauer and Wheaton 2006: 146). Although people who have been trafficked may identify as sex workers, trafficked people should not be conflated with people who choose to engage in sex work without being coerced (Butcher 2003). Sex trafficking, though, is enormous: between 700,000 and 1 million women and children are trafficked every year worldwide, and it is the third-largest source of organized crime, behind drugs and firearm trafficking (Schauer and Wheaton 2006).

Although cisgender men and transgender people engage in various forms of sex work, cisgender women are the focus of much discussion in research on sex workers, sex tourism, sex trafficking, and the sex work industry – and (cisgender) women are sometimes equated with sex work (see Scott and Minichiello 2014). In fact, sex work has largely been viewed through the lens of patriarchy, whereby sex work is seen as a product of gender inequality (Minichiello, Scott, and Callander 2013). The dominant focus on cisgender women (and minors) has oftentimes ignored cisgender men's and transgender people's participation in the sex trade (Weitzer 2009). Given this view of sex work as demonstrating gender inequality, academics have widely debated its exploitative nature mainly from the perspective of lack of rights and systematic abuses embedded in the more traditional notion of prostitution. For example, liberal feminists often call for the legalization of prostitution, arguing that sex work is *work*, and women should have the right to achieve economic gains through this profession (Beran 2012). On the other hand, radical feminists normally oppose the legalization of prostitution and see sex work, generally, as inherently disempowering and subjugating (Barton 2001; Chancer 1998; Chapkis 1997; Nagel 2003; Rubin 1993 [1984]; Taormino et al. 2013).

Aside from these feminist debates, most research on sex work, and specifically prostitution, has focused on sex work more as *sex* than work. Historically, sex workers were seen as vectors of diseases – mainly syphilis – and as public health threats (Wilson 2003; Minichiello, Scott, and Callander 2013). Today, a great deal of research still focuses on mental, physical, and sexual health interventions for sex workers, especially in the realms of HIV, risk, violence, and sexual victimization (Vanwesenbeeck 2001). Research explores the factors that contribute to whether sex workers use condoms or not, their drug use, and the cycles of violence in sex workers' lives (Vanwesenbeeck 2001; Surratt et al. 2004). HIV and drug use as related to sex workers' sexualities have come to be a mainstay of research into their lived experiences. In a way, a rehashing of old stereotypes and "moral panics" around sex workers being a threat to public health continues through this clinical mode, constantly researching and associating sex workers with HIV and other sexually transmitted infections.

Although the research on sex work is vast, we have tried to summarize some of its basic tenets in this section. There are various forms of sex work, legal or illegal, across different countries. Sex tourism and sex trafficking have emerged as major topics within the field of sex work, especially in a globalized world. Sex work has often only focused on gender inequality, and it has been framed through a patriarchal, gender-exploitative framework and/or a sexual public health framework.

Up to now, we have introduced different concepts of sex, sexual labor, sex work, and sex tourism, and how these categories of labor may indicate a negotiation of exploitation and agency simultaneously – and in ways more complex than offered in the media or by international NGOs. Now we explore the various (often conflated) aspects of trafficking on the one hand, and less-known erotic labor practices on the other, and how they relate to race. We do this analysis because, for us, race is intrinsically embedded in how sex work, desire, and erotic labor are co-constituted, in that a certain erotic currency is given to (or taken from) particular groups. We also tackle sexual trafficking separately to better engage in those discussions and to avoid contributing to the constant conflation of erotic labor and trafficking.

Complicating erotic practices: race in sex work

The picture painted in the previous section is often the general view of sex work, its framing, and its research agenda. However, in this section, we will begin to explore how race complicates and nuances one's understanding of sex work, sex tourism, and sex trafficking. This overview gives a racial perspective on sex work which sets the stage for the rest of this chapter, in which we offer an exploration of a more detailed examination of race and erotic labor. Sex work and erotic labor are inherently racialized, affecting how certain bodies experience sex work and erotic embodiment, how sex work unfolds in everyday life, and how issues around sex work are discussed in larger discourses. By unmasking how race is implicated within sex work, we propose a more complex understanding of the topic (outside of gender inequality) in order to push forward people's thinking about sex work, sex tourism, and sex trafficking today.

For the most part, racialization of erotic labor has been underdeveloped in sex work literature (Jones 2015). Nonetheless, race impacts erotic labor and sex work in very profound ways. Historically, in certain western countries, the figure of the prostitute was often associated with blackness and colonized people as a way to discipline white women to be sexually moral – to not be "those women" – and to subscribe to heterosexual marriage (McClintock 1992). Erotic "deviants" were figured as racial "deviants," reconstructing colonized people as having excessive, "primordial" sexualities (McClintock 1992). Laws against prostitution were also often used to try to force immigrants, the poor, and other women of color to assimilate into middle-class, white norms of chastity, marriage, and propriety (Lucas 1994). In this regard, the figure of the prostitute was racialized as non-white, marking whiteness as the proper sexual norm and casting people of color as sexual deviants (Ferguson 2004).

This stereotype is still often the rule in entertainment outlets: to see immigrant, mixed-race, Latina, Asian, and black sex workers is to construct whiteness as innocent and in contrast to people of color, portrayed as deviant. When risk and danger are associated with white (cisgender) women, the possibility of saving them is noteworthy (this pattern of saving white women continues to be the case even decades after the popular movie *Pretty Woman*).

Today, poor, black, immigrants, and other women-of-color sex workers are systematically exposed to harassment and violence by police (McClintock 1992). Women-of-color sex workers have fewer opportunities to work away from the streets and are disproportionately arrested for prostitution (Sloan and Wahab 2000). The private spaces of escort services are typically for white (cisgender) sex workers, whereby women-of-color sex workers (cisgender or transgender) are normally forced into public spaces (streetwalking) and are consequently exposed to more violence, stigma, and police presence (McClintock 1992 – see also Bernstein 2007). Also, despite the clients of sex workers in western countries being disproportionately white, middle-class, married men, these men are not policed and arrested (McClintock 1992). Instead, street prostitutes comprise a small minority of the people engaged in sex work, yet they make up 90 percent of those arrested, and those arrested are disproportionately women of color (Lucas 1994). In addition, white, middle-class men often hold racially stereotypical views and fantasies about escorts of color, making it harder for women of color to secure white men as their clients unless they enact and embody racialized sexual stereotypes for them (Minichiello, Scott, and Callander 2013).

An important method of countering the real financial obstacles experienced by women-of-color erotic laborers due to racialized sexual stereotypes is known as "illicit eroticism" (Miller-Young 2014). By deploying illicit eroticism, women of color become empowered to make use of their ostensible hypersexuality to garner increased profits in pornography, as well as in other forms of sex work. Through the deliberate reclaiming of racialized, sexualized tropes, women of color may carve a space for sex work to exist as a site of resistance and change. While these deployments of racialized sexual stereotypes have historically excluded women of color from spaces in which increased profit is possible (such as online escort services or high-end erotic dance clubs), the deliberate harnessing of erotic currency through racialized, sexualized imaginaries has the potential to communicate desirability and to result in increased profit.

As already stated, women of color have historically been cast as sexual deviants, and throughout early pornography, and even currently, have been made to embody figures such as the "voodoo priestess" or "jungle woman." Later in this chapter, we will explore the sexualized fantasies enacted by women of color in sex work, and how they are limited to racialized typecasting, whereas white women are able to embody boundless sexualized fantasy images, ranging from MILF (mother I'd like to f***) to cheerleader and nurse. Because of the presumed hypersexuality that women of color encounter in the sex industry, these other images are largely unavailable to them; women of color who are mothers are often portrayed as either "welfare queens," in the case of black women, or hypersexual immigrant mothers of "anchor babies," in the case of Latina women. The cheerleader imaginary embodies a sexual innocence unavailable to women of color, and the sexual character of the nurse assumes the character is educated, further implying that whiteness is the only racialized category associated with legitimate motherhood, innocence, and education.

Other issues exist in the realm of pornography as well. The rape and abuse of black women under slavery has linked sexuality with violence toward black women, which is still heavily characteristic of a great deal of porn today (Sloan and Wahab 2000). Black women in pornography are marginalized through an industry that pushes them to the periphery, where they are seen as disposable and/or fetishized through racialized stereotyping. However, black women can use this stereotyping of hypersexuality to achieve mobility and erotic autonomy within the sex industry (Brooks 2010; Miller-Young 2010). In this sense, people of color are often consigned to fetishized realms within pornography, based upon race-based sexual stereotypes (think about how, on porn sites, black/ebony, Asian, and Latina are categories, whereas white is not); nonetheless, people of color can also enact these stereotypes in order to obtain some monetary advantage in the sex industry (Brooks 2010).

Similar racial issues to those experienced by cisgender women play out for transgender sex workers as well. In examining sex work practices among different transgender communities in New York City, Hwahng and Nuttbrock (2007) found that African-American and Latina transgender women often engaged in street-based sex work, whereas Asian transgender women worked in apartments and hotels (see also Bernstein 2007). The same researchers showed that white cross-dressers often engaged in sex work for recreational purposes, rather than for survival like the transgender women of color in their study. Because of these contexts and reasons for engaging in sex work, Hwahng and Nuttbrock (2007) found, African-American and Latina transgender women were most "at risk" of contracting HIV, Asian transgender sex workers were at moderate risk, and white cross-dressers were at low risk. As one can see, race profoundly shapes how sex workers experience sex work, where they do it, and what challenges they face.

These issues have not gone away in the digital age either. For example, women of color often receive lower camscores when performing webcam modeling, thwarting their success in the online world of sex work (Jones 2015). Whiteness is privileged as bodily capital in the sexual marketplace, as online sex workers of color may have to rely on racialized sexual stereotypes in order to make a profit (Chin Phua and Caras 2008; Jones 2015). Chin Phua and Caras (2008) call this process "ethnic branding." In their study, male sex workers advertising their services online used "cultural packages" – stereotypes about a person of color's culture and appearance – in order to invoke a fantasy image in clients' minds. Ethnicity becomes commodified and fetishized as a personal brand in strategically marketing oneself. In another study on male sex workers, the researcher found that black men had the highest premiums when they were "tops" (sexual penetrators – a racialized sexual stereotype often associated with black men) and the lowest premiums when they said they engaged in "bottom" behavior (being sexually penetrated) (Logan 2010). Racialized sexual stereotypes shape bodily capital for sex workers, restricting them to making a profit only when they enact these race-based sexual "fantasies."

Within sexual tourism practices, whiteness is often privileged and bodies of color are "exoticized" through stereotypical fantasy tropes about hypersexual sexualities (Kempadoo 1996). Racist colonial hierarchies influence people's "preferences" for sex workers when engaging in sex tourism. Discussions on websites promoting the sexual services industry also engage in tropes commodifying the "exotic" and racial bodies through constructing women in Global South countries as "traditional" and subservient (Chow-White 2006). By contrast, in South Korea, white Russian sex workers, who serve as stand-ins for "western women," are usually the preferred sex workers in their renewed sex industry (Kim and Fu 2008). Again, within the realm of sex tourism, whiteness is privileged, and bodies of color are often only desirable if they are inscribed in and through colonial racist fantasies about hypersexuality and subservience.

Scholarship on women's participation in erotic labor has seldom foregrounded the experiences of women of color. When it has, a lack of attention has been paid to the consequences of the black/white racial binary in the United States in terms of how women of different ethno-racial groups become conceptualized along an either/or raced spectrum. For Latinas, Asians, and other women of color, this racial dichotomy causes a reductionist or sometimes absent reading of how ethno-racial identification is articulated through sexuality beyond blackness or whiteness. Women's participation in erotic labor, specifically dancing and pornography, is motivated by many factors, of which monetary compensation is foremost. The centrality of monetary compensation also pertains to other forms of erotic labor, such as that of sex tourism, sex trafficking, and "mail-order brides." In all such cases, access to high earnings and income potential are constantly mediated through race, as race-based sexual imaginaries make their way to the forefront of desire and the production of the erotic (Miller-Young 2014).

Within the realms of dancing and pornography, fantasy-based personas serve as temporal conduits through which women are able to embody sexualized characters and garner profit. These personas are fluid and can be modified according to the desires of clients and consumers, enacted through attire, hair, and makeup choices, among other things, and articulate a specific desirability. Race is a central determinant in the production of such personas, and in many instances it is not as fluid as other markers of sexualized character. Because the erotic is embedded in a field where desire is always already racialized, this profit is able to take many forms. Among such forms is the opportunity to self-promote through fantasy characterization, and, for women of color, specifically to make use of the ways one is imagined ethno-racially (Brooks 2010). This is not to say that women-of-color erotic laborers have an advantage when it comes to engaging in different kinds of sex work, but rather that the sexualized characterizations available to them are mediated and limited by race. These characterizations have the capacity to be commanded and articulated in ways that work to empower women of color (Miller-Young 2014).

Spotlight 4.1 Racialized Embodiments, Differential Treatment

This section complicates the homogeneous notion of "sex worker" by locating the distribution of racial and racialized readings onto different bodies. It opens with a conceptual situating of the very specific contexts of sexual and erotic labor that show this differential treatment and value when sex work is seen through racialized lenses.

Embodying sexualized fantasies

Common sexual imaginaries, such as that of schoolgirl, cheerleader, nurse, nanny, bride-to-be, and so forth, become parceled characters that are embodied and performed in erotic labor settings. Key to these performances are raced expectations around what kinds of bodies can and should depict such characters. For white women, there exists an implicit innocence associated with their erotic expressions, positioning them plausibly to embody fantasies related to young, naive, yet morally righteous fantasy characters. Whiteness, in this instance, becomes synonymous with propriety and is subsequently rewarded as ideal sexuality. For women of color, these characters are less available and less plausible when performed because of the ways in which women of color have been typified as dangerous, uncontrollable, and hypersexual. As noted before, black and brown people's sexuality is cast as deviant when juxtaposed with whiteness. Because race and sexuality are articulated through one another, racialized readings of black and brown women's sexuality have historically been associated with hypersexual, subservient, animalistic imaginations. Sexualized fantasies available to women of color, such as those of maid, housekeeper, gypsy, jungle woman, and so forth, are perceived to fit women of color due to racist, sexualized identifications of an assumed danger and perverseness associated with brown and black women's erotic expressions. This imaginary of black and brown women as subservient, hypersexual, and dangerous is reminiscent of colonial legacies where such ideas served as justification for rape and exploitation (Nash 2014; Collins 2004).

The nature of sexualized fantasy personas allows the existence of a relationship between appropriate bodies in terms of ethno-racial representations, but also, more broadly, bodies in general. In works regarding race and erotic labor (Brooks 2010; Maia 2012), features such as hairstyle/texture and skin color are regarded as racializing agents that produce specific imaginaries for erotic laborers and, more specifically, for dancers. Features of the body other than skin color and hair become racialized in the context of erotic labor, and inherently impact the availability to performers of certain sexualized personas. For example, the physical embodiment of the cheerleader fantasy relies on a white, thin/lean image lacking body hair, cellulite, stretch marks, and so on. Cheerleaders are considered innocent, young, and virgin, thus to apply the cheerleader persona to women of color, whose sexuality is typecast as opposite to this imaginary, would prove less successful. For black women, Latinas, and other women of color, the successful portrayal of racialized, sexed fantasies relies on reductionist imaginaries of stereotyped characterizations. Racialized scripts that exist around the body are shaped by their historicized experiences (Nash 2014).

The MILF phenomenon

Age has gained increasing importance as an identifier of desirability within pornography (Ogas and Gaddam 2011). How women in erotic labor come to be rewarded for embodying the sexual imaginary of the "MILF," first popularized by the US film *American Pie*, happens along raced and classed lines. For white women, being older and a mother are rewarded within pornography as sexually desirable traits. MILF videos depict MILF actresses as exercising agency, initiating sexual contact, and in control of sexual transactions. By way of this control being communicated on screen, MILF actresses are seen as occupying a high status – they are unquestioned, dominant, and frequently portrayed marking the bodies of young (white) men as disposable. This sense of control and agency in sexual transactions positions MILFs not only as seductive but also as defying traditional gender roles.

The capacity to defy gender roles and exhibit this level of control over white men is often inaccessible to women of color, who are commonly portrayed as being in sexual situations that involve coercion and subservience (Vannier, Currie, and O'Sullivan 2014). Women of color are rarely displayed exercising control over white men and, when they are, it typically involves a sense of control rooted in the exotic, mystified nature of the "third world woman" (Mohanty 1988). This imaginary is associated with women of color being sexual providers to the Global North, evident in how sexual tourism, trafficking, and "mail-order brides" are conceptualized and subsequently treated. This imaginary of coercion and subservience attributed to women of color becomes operationalized on a number of fronts, including public conceptualization of sexual tourism, sex trafficking, and "mail-order brides."

On sexual tourism

Despite its propensity for occurring in both the Global North and South, sexual tourism has been socially affixed as a product of the Caribbean, Asia, or specific parts of Latin America. Studies pertaining to how sexual tourism takes place in such areas have not accounted for the agentic practices of women and men who become involved in such labor or the many ways in which such labor occurs beyond the heterosexual and cisgender normative understandings (Kempadoo 2001). Erotic laborers in these regions are constructed as sexual providers to Global North tourists, reifying legacies of colonial dominance and subservience. Studies that focus on the production of sexual tourism have often relied on a homogeneous telling of the stories of sex workers and the circumstances they face in their home countries.

Sexual tourism takes many forms, including between same-sex individuals, women seeking men, men seeking women, and for the purposes solely of sex, as well as intimate and long-term relationships eventually leading to marriage.

On sex trafficking

Sex trafficking, which makes use of victim repair as a model for rehabilitating women who have been trafficked for sexual labor, benefits from the imaginary of these individuals as poor, disempowered, and victimized. Such an imaginary is based on racialized conceptions and an assumed lack of bodily autonomy pertaining to non-white women. By citing the constant need to "save" black and brown women from the pitfalls of sex trafficking, white, first-world feminists enact a savior paradigm that severely undermines the agency of the women whom they classify as "trafficked victims." This is not to say that all sex trafficking occurs under agentic circumstances in which participants are fully able to consent, but rather that sex trafficking is a diverse, nuanced practice that takes many forms. As such, to homogenize it and assume it occurs under the same circumstances of intimidation and coercion is too simplistic (Agustín 2007).

The history of "white slavery" can also be seen in the rhetoric around sex and human trafficking today. Historically, in the United States, "white slavery" referred to young white immigrant women and children who were lured from Ellis Island into brothels (Lucas 1994). White slavery in many Global North countries was often conflated with all forms of prostitution to generate a moral panic in order to end sex work. In these narratives, white women are constructed as "innocent" "victims" who are being exploited to perform erotic labor (Doezema 2000). This panic around "white slavery" has re-emerged in the discourse around the trafficking of women. The new discourse is also about youthful, "innocent" white women and is conjured up in order to make people fear immigrants and to again create moral panic around sex work (Doezema 2000). White women are constructed as the people who need saving from trafficking while, by the same process, all forms of sex work become stigmatized. Sex workers of color bear the brunt of this stigmatization as they are typically the most visible sex workers in the public sphere who are being criminalized.

On "mail-order brides"

The phenomenon of "mail-order brides" has roots in the picture bride system, in which photos of eligible women were sent abroad by families in an effort to arrange marriages with men. The ways in which women travel transnationally for the sake of marriage have since shifted dramatically as the "mail-order bride" industry has become extensive and lucrative. Such an industry is highly reliant on the economic necessity that makes women decide to enter the trade, as well as on the racialized, sexed stereotypes that follow the women who become involved in it. Frequently, Asian and Pacific Islander women are placed at the forefront of such discussions and typecast as embodying servility, subservience, and domestic skill ("old-fashioned" is also coded language for this imaginary). In addition to Asian and Pacific Islander women, women from Eastern Europe have also dominated the public conceptualization of who becomes involved in the bridal industry (Chun 1996).

The bridal industry utilizes the erotic imaginaries associated with Asian, Pacific Islander, and Eastern European women as a tool of proliferation. When they arrive in the United States or other receiving countries, brides experience multiple levels of racialization, including that of being a recent immigrant. This racialization and immigrant status, coupled with brides' dependence on their male husbands/partners to provide for them, carries the potential for different levels of coercion or exploitation.

Sex work and rescue industries, and sexual tourism – or globalized sex work

Critical studies on sex work and trafficking have slowly, but increasingly, emerged. Such work counters the simplistic narrative of victimization. In her book *Sex at the Margins: Migration, Labor Markets and the Rescue Industry*, Laura Agustín (2007) shows that the challenge is not what sex work and prostitution mean to people, but the ways in which the state's definition and boundary setting, previously interwoven with constructs of flow, transporting and traveling across borders, influence the migrant's actual experience – that categories such as business traveler, guest worker, refugee, or student carry specific travel sanctions that go under more or less surveillance. For Agustín, traveling through conduits of trafficking does not mean people are victims or that many migrants who engage in sex work are not expecting to stay (either in sex work or in the host country), but that the push–pull factors in migration are more complex than previously stated (this somewhat relates to Brazil's rural–urban international migration of sexual minorities; Parker 1999). Also, as noted before, the focus on female sex workers serves to frame the experience with migrant sex work as trafficked victims, erasing transgender people and cisgender male (heterosexual, bisexual, or gay) sex workers' experiences. Co-constituting the notion of victims who are trafficked is often unequivocally crafted – so much so that almost always we perceive them as victims who need to be saved. Agustín warns us against this liberal act which is really a psychological act of self-saving and, politically, an act that (often) excludes the immigrant through the figure of the sex worker.

Agustín's research into immigrant sex workers in Spain, and those from the rescue industries, is instrumental in pointing out the erroneous conflations between sex work and trafficking in relation to immigration and race. Because a lot of migrant sex workers are from Latin America, and not from other European countries or the United States, they are not seen as merely migrant workers but as temporary migrants – and in this, they are racialized. Her work also shows the erotic capital of the sex workers in these spaces. And she also demonstrates the temporality of the experience of those victimized due to their sex work experiences.

The moral panics around the global scale of trafficking (both real and imagined) have risen to levels of media coverage that collapse the differences between slave labor and exploitation, forced labor, human trafficking, sex trafficking, smuggling, prostitution, and sex work. In a BBC News debate in 2010, Agustín challenged international advocates, formerly trafficked persons, and Hollywood actors Mira Sorvino and Ashton Kutcher in their defense of these slippages.[5] The discussion of supposedly brainwashed trafficked people, whose interests are best served by a neocolonial gaze that attempts to tell them that what they experience is a full force of denial, is an important challenge to the tenets of sex trafficking discourse. Agustín shows force in her act of pushing back these neoliberally imposed (and inherently sociocultural readings of underdevelopment) views that already conflate all elements of the debate.

A discussion of sexual tourism may incorporate the power relations embedded in the choice of and access to travel of those who seek to pay for sexual transactions, or to solidify relationships from such encounters – encounters never devoid of power, with choices that are not innocent. However, travel, as noted before, produces a set of arrangements where the person migrating from the Global South is fully aware of the circumstances, is an active participant in the arrangement, and may indeed be engaged in such exchange for push–pull factors that benefit their family back home. Recent examples in popular media include the movie *Teddy Bear* (2012), featuring a man from Europe (in this case, an extremely shy bodybuilder from Denmark) traveling to an

Asian country for arranged relationships (in this example, with women from Thailand).

However, the case of someone from the Global North traveling to the Global South for sex tourism is not a neat binary – it happens in the United States, too (see Brents, Jackson, and Hausbeck 2010). There may be different types of sex markets within countries – ones that cater for sexual tourists but also others that cater for locals. Likewise, economic power, race, and gender can influence the dynamics of sex work and desire within Global South countries. Hoang's *Dealing in Desire* is a case in point.

In *Dealing in Desire*, Kimberly Kay Hoang (2015) also complicates notions of sex work, trafficking, and western hegemony. She shows the heterogeneity and complexities of the Vietnamese sex industry, detailing multiple markets catering to different clientele. These different markets, for Hoang, are shaped by the global economy – mainly the rise of certain Asian markets that have destabilized western hegemony. Within these markets, Hoang focuses on four groups of men and women and how race, gender, and sexuality unfold within the different spaces frequented by the men and the sex workers with whom each group of men interact.

The first group of men is the elite Vietnamese men, who are positioned at the top of the finance market. Sex workers are often crucial in helping elite Vietnamese men make business deals and become part of the display of conspicuous consumption that these men engage in. Within this space, the women would modify their bodies to perform a "pan-Asian modernity." The women often undergo nose jobs, wear makeup, have eyelid surgery, and practice other body modifications to present a modern Asian look – a look that is not western (e.g., no blonde hair and blue eyes) and modeled on Korean pop stars. This display and performance by sex workers bolsters elite Vietnamese men to perform a masculinity highlighting Asian ascendancy within the global financial markets.

The next group of men is the Viet Kieus, who are ethnically Vietnamese but who do not live in Vietnam. For the

Viet Kieus, the women present themselves as what Hoang calls "nostalgic cosmopolitan." This performance is more about displaying female deference, reifying a sense of an earlier Vietnam where women were more submissive. For the final two groups of men – western businessmen and western tourists/backpackers – the women perform "third world dependency." They darken their skin through tanning or makeup, get breast implants, and tell the men how poor they are. This performance enables men, who are seen as part of the declining western hegemony of global markets, to recuperate a sense of masculinity and reinvent themselves as neocolonialists. The white men also say that the women prefer their penises to the stereotypically small penises of Vietnamese men. This relies upon a wider sexual stereotyping of Asian men as not being masculine. The women who catered to the backpackers also engaged in more sexual intercourse for pay than the women who catered to other clientele.

These different markets show that sex work is heterogeneous and that notions of state, race, gender, and sexuality factor in desire and sex. Women adopt different racialized and gender embodiments in order to enable men to gain a sense of masculinity. For the elite Vietnamese, the women's "modern" look reaffirmed an Asian ascendancy. For the other men, the women perform deference and/or poverty to enable them to reassert their masculinities. Not only do these different performances and interactions reify certain racialized sexual and gendered stereotypes, they showcase how sex workers are social actors who are aware of what to perform and embody in order to satisfy their particular clientele.

Hoang shows how women also engage in rhetoric that challenges notions of trafficking and exploitation. These women even claim that they were more exploited when working in factories or as domestic laborers than they are as sex workers. Sex workers often worked in collaborative environments, so they did not perceive most of their work as dangerous. They did not see themselves as people who needed to be "rescued" by paternalistic NGOs but believed they had more autonomy now than in their previous occupations, as consent was essential to their current work and relationships. Notions of trafficking and exploitation need to be deeply questioned, then, as sex work is much more complicated than the often sensationalized accounts given around sex trafficking – accounts that often conflate trafficking with sex work and erase sex workers' voices.

Conclusion

This chapter has illustrated the complex relationship of erotic labor and sex work to race, and located it transnationally and globally through migration. We have shown the implications for the study of migration and race, gender and sexuality, and erotic labor by presenting a critical view of the literature on cisgender male-, cisgender female-, and trans-specific types of erotic labor that are largely intercepted by racial differences in a racial hierarchy that benefits white sex workers, giving them an advantage through readings of innocence; this is the very same system that explicitly chastises people of color, immigrants, and those who do not fit gender categories or social arrangements aligned with whiteness. Indeed, this work is part of a broader framework that questions the regulation of the use of public and semi-public spaces, but which also challenges citizenship and erotic labor, along with a range of other factors that are regulated in other sexuality topics (for more on that, see Bernstein and Schaffner 2005).

Racial and ethnic minorities, migrants, and people whose experience is not read as hegemonic in the Global North may experience a set of challenges unique to the nexus provided by the link between sex work/erotic labor and race. That fusion between the erotic and the roles of those who are in some way minoritized (whether in the United States or on a global scale) and who engage in sex work and erotic labor practices derives, in some analyses, from racial desire that not only configures racial arrangements but structures racist practices (Holland 2012). In significant ways, this chapter helps to conceptualize the scale of social value given to some, based on race and citizenship, to the detriment of the social readings of the rest. As well, it provides a challenge to reconceptualize discourses and experiences of and about sex work.

While this chapter has mapped sex work through migration, we turn in the succeeding chapter to examine how sexuality is co-constitutive of migration and immigration. We have shown how transnational human rights are bound up with race and sexuality and how sex work is always shaped by and through race. To make our final case, we turn to immigration, which is sometimes seen as racialized (if at all), to show how immigration is also shaped by and through sexuality.

5

Sexualizing Immigration

In the previous two chapters, our case studies have examined different aspects of race and sexuality. We situated the issues of gender, sexuality, and human rights discourses as more complex than a "West and the rest" racialized argument. We also produced an analysis of the complex and layered forms of erotic and sexual labor and how they are co-constitutive of a North/South divide that gets heavily racialized in particularly gendered ways. In this chapter, we want to ascertain the sexed, gendered, and sexualized forms in which the state regulates bodies, and how that surveillance/registering of oneself, as either newcomer or citizen, takes place through the racialized lenses of immigration politics (and markings of Otherness).

As this chapter will show, conceptualizing and describing the mutual constitution of immigration as race, and the gendered, sexual, and reproductive aspects of migration and race, is not necessarily a complex exercise – but it casts a critical eye in order to account for it. Multiple sources of gender/sexuality and migration/race explain this connection. For instance, in Cantú's *The Sexuality of Migration* (2009), the scholar asked: Does sexuality shape and organize all of migration?[1] Cantú took a simple, yet charged, message on a road sign alongside the main highway in Southern California (the Interstate 5 Freeway, between the San Diego and San Onofre border checkpoint) as a profound canvas for this analysis. The sign had a yellow-orange background, with a black silhouette that depicted three human beings. The generic figures represent an apparently undocumented family: leading is a man running, with a woman, smaller in size, running after him (clutching his hand – his body leads hers); at the same time, she is holding the hand of a young child who almost looks as if he is flying because of the representation of speed in the image. This sign is intended to make drivers aware of the possibility that (presumably undocumented) families may be crossing the wide highway as they cross the border, risking an accident, or even their lives, in the attempt. The impact of this figure was unpacked by Cantú as an always already heterosexual, but also reproductive, representation – one that serves as a threat to the USAmerican imaginary of immigration as a challenge to a hegemonically white country. By denoting the reproductive capacity deployed in images like these, the sign becomes a floating signifier of the weight of stereotypes – like the hyper-reproductive immigrant families that seek to settle in the United States through their children's right by US birth. In concrete ways, Cantú categorically states: "The sign is symbolic at multiple levels: a nuclear family unit, heteronormative in definition, a threat to the racial social order by virtue of its reproductive potential ... is also symbolic of the current state of international migration studies: sexuality is an implicit part of migration that has been overlooked or ignored" (2009: 118–19). Like Cantú, we have sought to continue to deconstruct the myriad ways in which gender and sexuality, and race and immigration, are often tied in constructions of Otherness in contemporary societies – by discussing the "down low" figures, or the construction of the racially erotic in sex work, or the challenges of a system that prioritizes certain narratives to produce citizenry and belonging through effeminacy linked to certain groups or hyper-masculinity in others.

Multiple accounts in the humanities and social sciences help demonstrate that migration processes and immigration are co-constitutive with race, gender, and sexuality. But immigration is often separated from race, and when immigration is read through race, sexuality is not evidenced (as in Cantú's previous illustration). Contemporary scholarship, activism, advocacy and policy work splits migration from the racial, or pursues an understanding of migration separate from gender and sexuality. We will make this argument clear by first presenting the various forms of migration and immigration, and highlighting their racialized (and sexualized) components in our opening section. We will then move to situate how different immigrant groups (in this chapter, we mostly focus on migration to the United States) experience migration, first by situating race and immigration, and adding to that policy, then gender, then sexuality, in order to demonstrate the multilayered accounts of this experience. From there, we will also address how immigration impacts and is impacted by sexualities, including sexual assumptions about immigrants, about sexual identities, and about sexual behaviors and desires. We close by briefly discussing the implications of this more complex understanding of migration and immigration. The principal purpose of this chapter is to illuminate how immigration and migration processes are formative of and formed by race and sexuality.

Context for the discussion of migration as racial (and sexual)

Migration is the movement of people from one place to another and the establishment of "a permanent or semi-permanent change of residence" elsewhere (Lee 1966: 49). As a social process, migration shapes multiple layers of the social, including the economic, political, cultural, environmental, health, and educational factors (as well as their effects). The need for migration was, and continues to be, documented as a tool for oppression and liberation for those fleeing challenges – economic or otherwise. These challenges are judged based on differences in cultural attributes, which often curtail political economic issues of core and periphery countries (and the administration of wealth and production within a world systems approach). To speak of migration requires that one conceptualize not just the migrant and refugee, but also the citizen and the deserving or entitled; thus to speak of migration is to speak of power, of nation, of access to citizenship, of the ways in which people are embedded in projects of expulsion or immersion, and of notions of the state granting the right to remain. One may migrate to a city, within a state or region, or engage in cyclical migration (that is, migration back and forth between "destination" and "origin" – troubling the understanding of both); one may also engage in migration to a different country (emigration speaks to the movement leaving a country/region/territory; immigration to the receptive country/region/territory in question).

Immigration is the international movement of people from one country to another; whereas internal migration is moving within one's own nation-state.[2] Voluntary migration is when individuals relocate because of their own personal desires, for reasoning that suggests that there are cost benefits to choosing migration, or because of the challenges faced in their countries of origin or residence. Forced migration, or displacement, is when individuals are coerced to move from their home region due to cultural, religious, structural, military, and other political factors – including prejudice against gender and sexuality of non-conforming people (or sexual minorities). Of course, the two are complex in their actual everyday occurrences; many people "voluntarily" migrate due to lack of access to minimal resources or with the hope of betterment at their destinations, so have really little or no incentive to stay, while others are "forced" to migrate via circuits of apparent trafficking but are intentionally using such conduits to leave their country of origin (Agustín 2007).

Likewise, migration is often seen within a set of push–pull factors framework (Tolnay and Beck 1990). Push factors can be economic, environmental, physical, social, or cultural (for instance, conflict, discrimination, and poverty can force an individual to migrate out of their current circumstances). Pull factors are based on elements such as economic opportunities, less discrimination in the desired destination, the presence of a regional or local network of family/extended family/chosen family/or other structures (not categorized through family nomenclatures), or even things such as a "better" environment (ranging from political climate to a perceived higher chance of productivity or social mobility), which attract people to the place that they are migrating to. Put another way, pull factors are based on the desirability of the new place of interest. Often, within an economic framework, migration is conceptualized as the act of being pushed out of poverty and pulled into an economy with more opportunities. However, as will be shown in this chapter, this framework is limiting because economics and migration are inherently bound up with notions of race and sexuality, and race and sexuality also add other layers of understanding to push–pull factors in migration. People do not migrate just because the Global North has something to offer people that the Global South does not (Luibhéid 2008b; Sassen 1992). Economic exploitation, colonial legacies, and military interventions create links and connections between countries, as well as stressors marked by racial, sexual, and gender components that underlie and co-constitute the processes and experiences of migration patterns for various groups.

Migration and globalization are inherently linked – in that the forms of thinking about who migrates, and why, establishes myriad ways of interpreting developing/developed countries and societies, with subsequent levels of respect for female embodied groups, acceptance of gender variance, and the embracing of sexual minorities. Migration also politicizes the countries of origin and their destinations, inherently producing democratic (and perceived to be more accepting) societies, in contradistinction from those who are portrayed as in need of the advancement of human rights (this is something we briefly discussed in chapter 3). Often, as in the case of Cuban Mariel immigrants to the United States (Peña 2013), the sexual and racialized readings were contrary to USAmerican norms of gender-conforming, white cisgender gay men. This clashing of the male normative, gay-affirming mainstream with Afro-Cuban effeminate (sometimes transgender) male-bodied individuals produced a racialized sexual migration that was region-, period-, and context-specific (as these Cuban immigrants' demographics were different from previous migration patterns from the same country).[3]

In effect, migration and immigration are complex processes bound up with economic, cultural, political, and a variety of other social factors. Globalization, international politics, and markets influence the flow of people within and between countries. However, gender and sexuality are also intimately tied to these processes of the movement of people, to which we now turn.

Sexual organization (and gender regulation) through race and immigration

This section begins with an illustration of race and immigration in USAmerican society, and of issues of power, in order to discuss US policy, along with gender, and then sexual, analyses. Our goal is to show the complexity of an analysis that dutifully incorporates all of these elements of a person's experience, as well as the multiple ways in which policy erases these structural relationships between variables. In showing how gender and sexuality are co-constitutive of migration and immigration, we offer up a more complex, nuanced, and complete picture in order to consider these practices and processes in a new light.

Race and immigration: a brief, historical overview

The United States is often depicted as a nation of immigrants, with the Statue of Liberty symbolizing this melting-pot imaginary (Kibria, Bowman, and O'Leary 2014).

However, the assumption often underlying this notion of the immigrant nation is the idea that immigrants will assimilate into "mainstream" (read: white) culture. In this manner, the immigrant is connected to a notion of becoming de-raced by passing through a conduit of acceptance by the "host" culture (though really the pressure amounts to assimilating notions of whiteness). Whiteness becomes invisible, while at the same time central, to the lens that produces citizenship and belonging. Ironically, there are ways in which one can achieve a "look" of legality, of having passed through a system, or having been examined by an immigration officer (Epps 2001). Through an assimilationist imperative, race can be "overcome," and one becomes simply an "American" or a "citizen." This notion of the USAmerican or "proper" citizen is racialized, in that it is centered on white hegemonic discourse and practice. A colorblind discourse around immigration and racism is engendered, in which immigrants are seen as either law abiding ("acceptable") or not (Kibria, Bowman, and O'Leary 2014). If one is an acceptable immigrant, citizenship may be achieved. Yet citizenship is never innocent, and to achieve citizenship is to find a passage through a legal system that simultaneously connotes how there were many who did not achieve it – those who died or were beaten or faced other forms of violence, as well as those who neither moved nor migrated (Epps 2001).

As mapped out below, however, this colorblind discourse has a long history of immigration linked to processes of racialization that cannot be separated or de-raced, especially given the history of immigration laws and the exploitation of migrant labor in the United States and other Global North countries. Despite the myriad ways that tolerance is projected as a fundamental ideal embodied in the Global North, immigrants face an assimilationist imperative, the root cause of which is meant to pacify the racialized anxieties of receiving communities. Oftentimes, the preconceptions about immigrants that catalyze these anxieties exist at the intersection of race and sexuality and are sustained by compulsory whiteness.

Racial divisions shape and are shaped by immigrant experiences. Kibria, Bowman, and O'Leary (2014) coin the term the "race-immigration nexus" to capture how ideologies, institutions, and practices come together to link race and immigration. Global North countries have always needed labor from abroad; however, the political, economic, and cultural conditions that shape migration flows and settlements are often effaced within these specific focuses on economic processes (Kibria, Bowman, and O'Leary 2014). In this chapter, we illustrate these other processes, especially their racial, sexual, and gender intertwining and co-constitutive components: in other words, our point of departure is the links between these aspects that are camouflaged by a cultural defense of the more comprehensive human rights found in the host society (as noted in chapter 3) which conceal its economic-driven policy-making efforts. We see, for instance, very specific racialized jobs for immigrants as part of a hierarchical chain of labor (much of it exploitative and without any labor rights) coded as "opportunity" for those whose lives in their countries of origin may not, in the eyes of the privileged, have amounted to much (for more on this, see especially Kibria, Bowman, and O'Leary's "Chapter 3: Race and the Occupational Strategies of Immigrants").

Race and immigration have historically been ways to sustain a subordinate surplus population that serves particular roles, from the assignment of temporary immigration status to Chinese laborers/workers in the nineteenth century to the very specific legal claims of immigrants (successful in their own right, either as owners of businesses or in respectable white-collar professions) who were unable to claim whiteness in the early twentieth century. Race control, whiteness, and the full-lived benefits of citizenship are countered (and in some ways the other side of the coin) by the "Othered" side: that of the non-white immigrant (mainly, today, the brown immigrant), the undocumented, the refugee, as well as the mutilated women, the gender non-conforming, and the gay, lesbian, or trans asylum seekers.[4]

Race, immigration, and US policy

The trajectory of US immigration policy demonstrates the significance of race in shaping the immigrant experience, writ large. Kibria, Bowman, and O'Leary (2014) define three different eras in immigration policy in the United States: restriction, reform, and enforcement. All three of these are tied to racial formation and the need for immigrant labor while maintaining nativist sentiments.

Laws governing immigration to the Global North have historically fed the demands of capitalism. When Chinese workers began to be seen as a threat to white men, restrictions were imposed with the 1882 Chinese Exclusion Act – the first law to exclude a particular group of people from the United States. Chinese immigration was seen as an evil, an "unarmed invasion" (Lee 2002). In a series of attempts to criminalize Chinese immigrants, opium, a fairly popular drug amongst Chinese immigrants, was outlawed. This process relied on the assumption that Chinese men would corrupt white men and women by making the drug easily accessible to them. The Chinese Exclusion Act prohibited Chinese laborers from immigrating to the United States for ten years and prevented them from obtaining legal citizenship. Not only did this law exclude people by ethnicity, but it also barred a group of people based on their class in that Chinese *laborers* were excluded, but not other groups, such as Chinese diplomats, teachers, and merchants (Lee 2002; see also Sears 2015). Essentially, this law set in motion the legalization and reinforcement of the need to restrict "undesirable" immigrants – where undesirable is coded as and measured by not living up to whiteness, threatening the white racial order, and/or not assimilating into white culture.

Spotlight 5.1 Clare Sears's *Arresting Dress*: Stereotypes Influencing Policy Making

Published in 2015, Clare Sears produced a provocative historical reading of how the law, social norms, and the migratory processes of workers were fused in the regulation of gender and other social crossings (cross-dressing as a term was used at the time specifically for gender-coded clothing and accessories). Based on San Francisco's laws in the second half of the nine-teenth century, Sears demonstrates how cross-dressing and cross-gender behavior were acts of defiance that proliferated in semi-public and private spaces: parties, semi-private theater "freak" shows, and other spaces that could be controlled in terms of access, yet could be raided by the police. In showing this archival-based engagement with social norms and the law, *Arresting Dress* denotes the beginning of a nuanced gender dif-ferentiation that promoted control through punitive legal processes of male-bodied individuals who cross-dressed in ways that defied modernity and nation as articulated through perceived and normative mascu-linity and maleness. Interestingly, those same decades showed much more tolerance for clothing-based gender bending engaged in by female-bodied individuals. Some female-bodied individuals cross-dressed in public, and their appropriation of certain spaces allowed them to work in the mines, or temporarily occupy those spaces socially perceived as masculine (although in some situa-tions they lived as men more permanently). The state's investment in regulating gender is perhaps best demon-strated by the fact that female-bodied individuals who behaved this way often did still get arrested.

Cross-dressing regulations acted principally to control gender-specific roles and to produce social norms of "decency" that reproduced two genders and sustained a heteronormative system. Sexuality and gender were coded in these binary normative terms, even though categories of sexual orientation and gender iden-tity had not been solidified in the USAmerican imagi-nary of gender (and sexuality). Private parties where male-bodied individuals cross-dressed allowed them to dance with male-bodied individuals whose gender presentation was masculine, thus co-producing gender difference (and a sexual-attraction differentiation). But the latter is something Sears describes as non-normative sexual practices in order to disentangle gender presentation from sexuality and sexual activity or desire, while at the same time affirming gender and sexuality's intimate relationship. The author rightly refuses to use "gay and lesbian" identities, which would be a historical misplacement and a reduction of broader historical elements to more contemporarily relevant categories. In response, Sears coins the term "trans-ing analysis" to demonstrate multidisciplinary efforts to read these historical attempts at gender regulation, but without attributing these to either gender identity or sexual orientation.

More to the point here, *Arresting Dress* demonstrates the connections between immigration and race, and gender and sexuality, by illustrating the place of Chinese immigrants in these imaginaries of oppositional genders/sexualities/races. There were festivals and theaters where tourist "slumming" took place, and in many instances cross-dresser "freak" shows were put on in Chinese neighborhoods. The "problem bodies" that the author speaks of are the bodies of those who existed in the dark space of social exclusion, bodies that were read as anatomically distinct. According to Sears, "slumming" tourists wanted to explore the bodies of Chinese women, believing there were inherent differences between white and Chinese female bodies; other tourists gazed at the feminine presentation of Chinese men as part of a "spectacle for tourist consumption" that Sears calls "dehumanizing scrutiny" (2015: 113). Gender crossings, cross-dressing, and racial/immigrant experiences fused together in the conception of otherness to construct the imaginary of difference that made the immigrant, the non-white, the gender fluid, and gender non-conforming (whether cross-dressed or not) the opposite of normative.

In the final analysis, Sears's argument is a compelling transdisciplinary approach that demonstrates how the gender (and sexual) regulation of cross-dressing that took place in San Francisco (which affected anyone who cross-dressed) served as a platform on which to "mobilize support for federal immigration laws that excluded Chinese migrants from the nation" (140–1). *Arresting Dress* shows how the deployment of these control mechanisms, launched as they were by cultural anxieties, depended on an image of femininity (or more explicitly, hyperfemininity) that attached to Chinese men, converting these independent instances into a more coherent cultural narrative – a moral panic – that still has repercussions today.

Arresting Dress (2015) is not an isolated research project documenting these racial and sexual forbidden crossings. To situate whiteness as oppositional to men of color was a strategy of resistance that scholars such as Kitch (2009) denounce as "sexual projection." Chinese, Mexican, and black men were targeted during the late nineteenth and early twentieth centuries as part of racial/sexual control – where white men did not only want to prevent black men from having sexual intercourse with white women, they also lynched Mexican and Chinese men (and some women) for crossing these lines. Sometimes the framework of projection took on a heterosexual racial transgression; at other times, perceptions of some of these non-white men carried hegemonic notions of sexuality, sexual purity, and non-intermingling. Thus, once again, masculinity, maleness, and nation are in synchronization, sustaining the nation as white and deserving, and the rest as excluded from symbolic or actual citizenry.

After the 1882 Chinese Restriction Act, restriction continued through the National Origins Act of 1924 that consolidated whiteness through the creation of the "illegal immigrant." "Illegal" immigration meant that someone was a foreign national in the United States without legal authorization (Kibria, Bowman, and O'Leary 2014). The terms "legal" and "illegal" recode immigration status as individual indicators of morality, effectively obscuring the racial fears and tensions underlying international migratory process and experience (Luibhéid 2008b). As stated earlier, "(il)legal" immigration folds into a colorblind discourse, where certain racialized groups (nowadays Latinas/os, specifically Mexicans in the United States; often Muslim immigrants in many Western European countries) are targeted for supposedly not obeying the law and/or cultural values of the Global North country, concealing the racial undertones and tensions that prompt nativist sentiments.

Reform came about with the 1965 Immigration and Nationality Act that lifted discriminatory national-origin quotas, allowing for the growth of a more diverse foreign-born population. This act, motivated by egalitarianism, eased restrictions on Asian immigration as well as on other groups such as Eastern Europeans (Chin 1996). Nonetheless, while Luíbheid (1997) shows that racial and ethnic preferences were no longer explicitly codified in immigration law, so-called neutral criteria of the seven preference categories (e.g., unmarried sons and daughters of US citizens; members of the professions and scientists; and artists of exceptional ability) were raced, classed, gendered, and sexualized. The "neutral" criteria were based on notions of an abstract individual (male, white, middle-class, heterosexual, and unattached), so that individuals deviating from these norms could be excluded.

Enforcement, which characterizes the current era, began in the 1970s with the fear of "unauthorized" immigrants (Kibria, Bowman, and O'Leary 2014). The Immigration Reform and Control Act of 1986 penalized anyone who employed undocumented workers. A decade later, the Illegal Immigration Reform and Immigrant Responsibility Act increased border personnel and made it harder for undocumented immigrants to access social safety nets. Indeed, US border patrols employ racial profiling targeted at particular ethnic and racial groups (Acosta 2008; Kanstroom 2007).

Since September 11, 2001, this profiling and expansion of immigration control has focused heavily not only on Mexicans and other Latinas/os but also on Muslim and Middle Eastern immigrants.

Outside of immigration, racial processes of migration have been unfolding within the US nation-state as well. For example, black migration and urbanization fully began at the turn of the twentieth century (Tolnay and Beck 1990). Although economic opportunities are often seen as the main force driving black migration to the urban centers and the US North, both economic and social factors influenced these migratory processes. Racial violence in the South, especially mass lynching, was a contributive cause of black migration. Northern employers also sought to exploit cheap black labor, and there was a sharp drop in Eastern European immigrants at the same time (Tolnay and Beck 1990). More recently, during Hurricane Katrina in New Orleans, Louisiana, almost the entire population of the city was displaced. However, whiter and wealthier people had enough social and economic capital to return (Fussell, Sastry, and VanLandingham 2010). Black people lived in areas subject to the worst flooding and suffered more housing damage, which led to their delayed return or, for many, no return at all in a process that started much earlier than Katrina, which Thomas (2014) refers to as "racialized disaster." As can be seen, economic, social, and cultural racial processes impact internal and forced migration as well.

Gender, race, and immigration

Before examining further how immigration, race, and sexuality are interlinked, it is important to note the initial feminist interventions that revealed how gender, race, and immigration are mutually co-constitutive (see, among others, Hondagneu-Sotelo 2003; Kitch 2009). Originally, within immigration scholarship, academics often just studied women's migration experiences without paying any attention to how power and gender inequality shape and are shaped by these migratory experiences. In fact, even now, policy and economy analysts from the World Bank and the International Monetary Fund frame the international movement of women as a mere economic or human rights-driven migration (Morrison, Schiff, and Sjöblom 2008; for the latter, see also Rubio-Marín 2006). This approach ignores the relational effect of power and gender. Eventually, gender was recognized as essential to social practices that shaped migration patterns. In turn, migration was seen as reconfiguring gender relations and inequality. For example, women who migrate can become the breadwinners for their families, reconstituting their role within the household. Gender is a key constitutive element of migration (Hondagneu-Sotelo 2003).

The contributors to the anthology *Global Woman* show how women in the Global North rely on women from the Global South to perform care work in order for Global North women to gain financial independence (Ehrenreich and Hochschild 2002). The organization of care through migrant labor works to define women from the Global South as givers and those from the Global North as receivers. Global North women entering the workforce need someone to do care work – the *pull* factor – while poverty forces many women in the Global South to leave there and take over care work – the *push* factor. Racial stereotyping of women from the Global South as "naturally" good care workers eclipses the emotional work and labor that these women perform. By characterizing domestic labor as unskilled but intrinsically rewarding, transnational domestic laborers, who are usually women, become seen as "naturally" having a level of emotional intimacy with receiving families. This sense of intimacy produces unequal power dynamics that oblige workers to perform emotional labor by way of expressing their indebtedness to receiving families.

Gender, then, is not just a variable to add to immigration. Gender shapes economic displacement and demand in that women are seen as cheaper and more subservient employees (Pessar 2003). Women may gain economic independence, but whether they are "empowered" is less clear because new forms of oppression are engendered. For example, men may abuse their breadwinner wives because they perceive this new status as a threat to their masculinity.

With regard to gender and (hetero)sexuality, Mexican women who have migrated to the United States have taught their daughters more egalitarian views of sexuality, showing how (hetero)sexualities can be altered as a result of migration (González-López 2003). Exposure to US mainstream culture and society has transformed the sex lives of some Mexican immigrant women (González-López 2005) who have become critical of sexual ideologies that were instilled in them in their country of origin as well as by their families. González-López's research reveals the connection between the sex lives and choices of immigrant women and their relocation. By obtaining agency through the trials of immigrating, González-López finds that immigrant women take control over their intimate lives. Mexican immigrants often have to practice the "Taylorization" of sex – scheduling sex into their busy lives. Heterosexual Latinas also gain economic leverage, which can lead to more egalitarian relationships and autonomy in procreative decisions (González-López 2005). Migration, then, can change the way people, especially women, negotiate and navigate their intimate relationships.

Sexuality, race, and immigration

Much like gender, sexuality has been proven to be a constitutive aspect of migration, rather than a mere variable. Cantú's entry point to this chapter serves as a good compass to situate the academic terrain where sexuality and immigration meet. In queering the standpoint on immigration, one can see the heteronormative practices and processes that have shaped immigration policies and immigrant experiences. Sexuality can affect the decision to migrate, how the migratory process unfolds, and how one adjusts to life after migrating (Asencio and Acosta 2009). Likewise, identities that immigrants migrate with can shape, and are shaped by, immigrant experiences as well (Cantú 2009).

The term *sexual migration* is thus used to capture migration processes based on people's sexuality (Carrillo 2004; Asencio and Acosta 2009). As stated already, economic-labor models of migration overlook social factors; and, for the purpose of our argument in this section, those models ignore elements such as sexual freedom and gender equity (Asencio and Acosta 2009). Sexual migration offers a critique of the straightforward push-and-pull economic understandings of migration (Howe 2007). Another relevant term in this discussion is *Sexilio*, or sexile, coined by Manolo Guzmán (1997) to address the pressures on (often middle-class) families whose sons or daughters are gay or lesbian. These offspring may be temporarily "shipped" to US universities and employment from their countries (in Guzmán's example, Puerto Rico) so that the families do not have to deal with the presumed shame of their child's non-normative sexuality. Sexual migration and sexile approaches to the study of sexual minorities' migration depict a complicated relationship to structures of family, gender negotiations, and perceptions of sexuality (see also Acosta 2013).

The category "homosexual" was brought into being partly through the policies and regulatory mechanisms of the state (Canaday 2009). These policies explicitly used (homo)sexuality to define who could not enter the country, and hence homosexuality was created not just by medical and psychiatric institutions but also by immigration law. During the early 1900s in the United States, the Braun Report called for sodomites to be deported (Canaday 2009), and in 1917 the explicit exclusion of gay and lesbian migrants was encoded in measures that excluded those who were seen to engage in behaviors categorized as "crimes of moral turpitude" (Howe 2007). These sexual "perversions" were classed and racially coded as well, in that deviant sexual behaviors were seen as behaviors of the poor and/or people of color (Canaday 2009). In effect, perversion was seen as an act, and perversion was encoded in law onto the immigrant body. In the 1950s, however, homosexuality began to be separated from race and class, appearing to pose its own distinct threat to the nation-state. Moving away from just sexual behavior, the McCarren-Walter Act of 1952 explicitly barred homosexuals from entering the United States. In 1965, US immigration laws were reworded to exclude "sexual deviates," and until the late 1980s US immigration continued to disallow homosexuals (Manalansan IV 2003).

Today, US immigration laws still bar certain sexual minorities and other people based on their sexuality. There are still HIV bans, narrow definitions of families, and rigid asylum policies that keep certain sexual minorities from migrating to the United States and other Global North countries (Luibhéid 2004). Indeed, preventing people living with HIV from entering a country is part of this longer history of people's fears of migrants, their sexuality, and their disease (Howe 2007). To uphold family ties as the most important type of social relationship, friends were dropped from immigration laws in the 1890s. In turn, family was reinscribed as spouse and children, and family was meant to maintain white racial order and to prevent intra-racial relationships. Class, again, shaped these processes; if one did not have specific family ties to facilitate migration, one had to have a high degree of human or economic capital to be preferred under US immigration law (Luibhéid 2008b). The Uniting American Families Act was introduced in 2013 in order to try to unite binational same-sex partners; however, it was not until the federal legalization of same-sex marriage that binational same-sex couples could use marital family ties to enable a spouse to immigrate.

Gay identity itself is also characterized by internal migration, often (especially for white gay identity) involving migrating away from the family and to urban enclaves (D'Emilio 1993). People migrate out of certain areas in order to avoid anti-gay sentiments, sodomy laws, and/or anti-gay violence (Asencio and Acosta 2009). The Global North discourse on gay and lesbian culture and identity can also affect migratory practices (Manalansan 2003). Globalization and transnationalism impact and are impacted by identity formations. Homosexuality is different in Global North contexts than elsewhere, where immigrants confront "coming out" and the closet differently. Immigrants who do not disclose their non-heterosexuality are seen to have internalized homophobia and to not be the "normal" gay subject (Decena 2011). However, coming out may be understood tacitly within certain immigrant families and communities. For some immigrants, however (specifically Dominicans to the United States in Decena's study), embracing a gay identity allows them to feel "modern" and "progressive." The immigrant men in Decena's study linked gay identity with upward mobility. Sexuality, then, becomes, for some, an assimilation tool to distance oneself from one's Dominicanidad.

Migrants may experience new forms of inequalities and opportunities (Luibhéid 2008a). In Asencio and Acosta's (2009) study, lesbian Latinas who migrated away from their families gained certain forms of sexual autonomy; however, they experienced new forms of race and class prejudices (see also Acosta 2013). Although sexuality was not a main factor in their choice to migrate, it became an explanation for their not wanting to return (Asencio and Acosta 2009). Essentially, sexual autonomy and certain forms of social mobility were gained, but at the expense of an increase in their racialized identity.

Lesbian as a category is often a slippery one in immigration proceedings and research, the law, and the discussions around policy and human rights. Indeed, Eithne Luibhéid (2002) connects the Asian immigrant sex worker and lesbian women (whether gender non-conforming or not) as some of the subjects that are regulated by the state through immigration control. In her analysis of how sexuality, along with class, gender, and race, interact in order to serve as a filter of immigration access, all are subjects produced as threats to the state. At a more macro level, as Luibhéid (2002) shows, lesbian women are proxy for racial/immigration readings that reduce their migration to "better lived experiences," or punish them for being unfit within the receiving country, but also, in some other ways, undeserving of migration due to their gender transgressions. And at the more interaction and micro levels, as Acosta (2013) shows, sexually non-conforming Latinas must negotiate their relationship to the family and their immediate environment in ways that simultaneously erase their sexuality but reify a more traditional construction of gender and gender expression.

It is essential to note that not all people who migrate have homogeneous understandings of same-sex desire (Carrillo and Fontdevila 2014). LGBT immigrants may change their desires, practices, and partners post-migration, but these changes are not uniform. People do not simply shift from "pre-modern" to "post-modern" notions of sexuality – notions often based on Global North definitions of sexuality. Instead, identities, practices, and desires become hybrid constructions through the migratory process. For example, for some Mexican gay migrants, *activo/pasivo* and object-choice gay paradigms are combined (Thing 2010). Ethnic and immigrant identities can make their sexual identities less salient once in the United States.

Sexuality and immigration also work differently in different contexts. For example, women from the Global North who moved to Shanghai experienced upward economic and social mobility but downward sexual mobility (Farrer and Dale 2014). People can experience sexual marginalization and/or desexualization as they move across different cities and countries. In Farrer and Dale's (2014) study, white women from the Global North gained financially by migrating to Shanghai but were often masculinized and seen as non-desirable in their new Global South context.

As we can see, sexuality deeply impacts and is impacted by migration. People may migrate because they experience sexual oppression in their country of origin. When people migrate, their views on and about sexuality, sexual behaviors, and other sex-related matters may change as well. Migration can therefore change sexual status and sexual desire. Migration itself to urban centers is often credited with the rise of (white, middle-class) gay identity and communities within the United States and other countries. Essentially, migration and sexuality are intimately tied into how and why people migrate and how and why migration may influence people's sexuality before, during, and afterward. Aside from how this movement and sexuality are related, immigration and sexuality are also connected in the way in which immigrants, like many people of color, experience sexual stereotypes.

Sexual stereotypes of immigrants

"When Mexico sends its people, they're not sending their best. [...] They're bringing drugs. They're bringing crime. They're rapists." A now famous quote, from then presidential candidate Donald Trump, highlights the stereotyping of certain immigrant groups in the United States. Mexican immigrants, as well as immigrants from other Latin American countries such as Colombia, have been stereotyped as hyper-masculine drug dealers and hypersexual rapists. These stereotypes (used effectively enough to win the presidency) rely upon wider ones in the white imagination that see Latinas/os as exotic and passionate, especially those with darker skin (González-López 2006; Brooks 2010). However, used in the contexts of immigrants, these create an us-versus-them mentality. The immigrants are bad, enacting bad forms of sexuality and sexual behaviors, and the United States is good and needs to protect itself from these bad immigrants (or "bad hombres" as Trump later called them). These discourses completely obliterate the facts: stereotypes are not empirically true, and people in the United States bring plenty of drugs, crime, and rape to their own country. Indeed, rape was used as a weapon by the colonizers against Native Americans and slaves. Sexual stereotyping, though, has been allowed to stop certain groups from entering the country.

For example, when Asian immigrants, and especially Chinese immigrants, were the focus of American fears, sexual stereotyping was also used to demonize them. In the first wave of migration to the United States, East Asians were seen as hypersexual (Chua and Fujino 1999). Such clichés stemmed from a longstanding concept of East Asia as the "exotic Orient" (Said 1978). In constructing East Asia as exotic, the Global North could position itself as the "normal" modernized culture. The Fu Manchu characterization also helped portray East Asians as sly, cunning, and cruel. During World War II, Japanese immigrants and Japanese Americans were considered sexual threats to white women. Having obtained a higher status through assimilation, Asian immigrants, especially men, were then portrayed as asexual and emasculated, seen to be doing "women's work," such as launderers and domestic servants, and hence were constructed as beneath white US citizens and sexually non-threatening to white women (Chua and Fujino 1999; Han 2006b). Sexual stereotyping – first hypersexual and later asexual – has been used to dehumanize East Asian immigrants and to legitimize excluding them from entering the country.

The racialized and sexualized discourses that propagate the notion that people of color, and particularly women of color, are hypersexual are also exemplified in the case of the sterilization of Puerto Rican women and other women of color. Sterilization was first practiced in 1901, when the island's poverty was attributed to overpopulation. Following its implementation, the racialized tenets of the practice became evident when it was found that disproportionate numbers of poor and uneducated women were sterilized, often without their consent. The assumption in Puerto Rico was that poor women were hypersexual, producing children at the expense of the state, when in reality the sterilization campaign benefited US economic interests (Lopez 1993).

In the Global North, Arab immigrants are typecast as well. Arab men are seen as hypersexual, dark, and threatening, especially in Western European countries such as France where there is a large immigrant Arab population from North Africa (Cervulle 2008). In a post-9/11 era, these stereotypes have also conflated being Arab with being Muslim, and this discriminates against even those wrongly believed to be Muslim, such as Sikhs (Puar 2007). Arab women are also hypersexualized because of practices such as belly dancing, in which they appear veiled, yet scantily clad (Maira 2008). These stereotypes are used to legitimize violence against Arab people within Global North countries, to ban them from immigrating, and to justify western imperialism against Arab countries.

All of these sexual stereotypes work to not only legitimize countries in the Global North as possessing "normal" (read: white) sexuality, but also to effectively dehumanize immigrants and justify their exclusion. Sexual stereotyping of immigrants, then, is a discursive strategy that historically and currently demonizes immigrants who are constructed as a threat to the western nation-state. Joane Nagel coined the term "ethnosexual intersections" to contextualize the co-constitutive nature of ethno-racial identity and sexuality, and traces the hypersexualization of people of color to "forbidden frontiers," which motivate white men and women to seek out sexual relationships with people of color because of the fetishized nature of such relationships.

Citizens who are understood as deviant and threatening to the western nation-state are also policed on a domestic level, as evidenced by the work of Angela Onwuachi-Willig in her 2013 text, *According to Our Hearts: Rhinelander v. Rhinelander and the Law of the Multiracial Family.* Onwuachi-Willig argues that, although it currently seems that interracial couples are not subject to discrimination in the United States, this assumption is far from accurate. She coins the term "interraciality" to refer to the discrimination experienced by interracial couples. Her work finds that the willingness to enter into an interracial relationship threatens whiteness and provokes anxiety. Onwuachi-Willig centers black/white relationships by focusing on the case of *Rhinelander v. Rhinelander* where a wealthy white man tried to annul his marriage because of his wife's status as a mixed-race person. Onwuachi-Willig examines this case in an effort to show that, despite the relative gains made on behalf of interracial families and couples, those with a black partner face excessive discrimination. In effect, racialized sexual stereotypes work locally and globally to deem who is worthy and who is not to enter and remain in society or to travel freely around the world.

Conclusion

Immigration, race, sexuality, reproductive rights, and gender are all interconnected in critical ways. This chapter has aimed to show how the relationship between sexuality and race is operationalized through the lens of migration, immigration, and transnational processes and, just as importantly, through the gaze that regulates and organizes populations in hierarchical ways. We have challenged that gaze and the Global North/Global South dichotomy, while situating our work within those terms. And we have shown the power of racialized practices that take sexuality as a basis for constructing oppositional realities. The sexual stereotypes of non-white immigrants sustain a division between the groups, maintaining a hegemonic reading from the position of USAmericans and incurring the misreading of immigrants as dangerous.

The chapter has also mapped out a historical trajectory that problematizes assumptions of belonging and citizenship by looking at the constant negotiations of many immigrants, and their evacuation from the symbolic arrangements of society, as in the case of Chinese workers. That exclusion from resources and citizenry has continued right into the twenty-first century, allowing the advancement of a neoliberal agenda of control and deportation. Now, more than ever, it is important that the connections between the racialized and sexual are made visible, so as to propose forms of resistance to the conservative backlash in many parts of the world.

Our conclusion will discuss the implications of this and previous chapters in order to suggest future work and policy impact.

Conclusion: Racialized Sexualities – On Experience, Policy, and Scholarship

This book started with a provocation: we defended our position that, no matter the area of study, race and racialization processes cannot be considered independently of sexuality (and within that, processes of gendered sexualities), and sexuality and sexualization processes cannot be seen as detached from race. We also insist that the framework of racialized sexualities is critical in the study of social life, from the most mundane to the institutional and structural, and to the discourses that impact contemporary societies. The goal of this book has been to bring together a set of disparate topics and literatures that converge in making racialized sexualities a potentially fruitful, continuously evolving, though still young, field of study.

The chapters that served as our case studies are only the beginning of such explorations. We foresee further work in the areas of criminal justice, health, media, religion, education, the impact of homelessness, erotic labor beyond sex work, employment and promotion/retention, the military, and on issues and topics like aging, multi-raciality, consumer analyses, science, communications and marketing, neighborhoods, urban studies, gentrification issues, and overall areas of inequality – locally, nationally, and transnationally.

Race and Sexuality has provided a more nuanced analysis about the relationship between these two powerful categories – historically, conceptually, and in everyday life – using case studies both in the United States and comparatively and transnationally. Because we see the potential in the argument for thinking about race and sexuality together, we have considered many cases from popular media and incorporated examples from social scientific research in order to support our argument. Readers will leave the pages of this book with a clearer understanding of the linkages between race (and class) and sexuality (and gender). Our argument shows how race and sexuality operate in and through each other, and that an analytics of racialized sexualities is more common than previously discussed in the scholarship.

Yet, and as importantly, we wish to convey that even when these two categories are not obviously "matched" in a given social, political, or cultural issue, the configuration of their relationship must be borne in mind, even when one is more salient than the other. Take the quest to regulate sex work. In sex work, racial undertones are often covert, and the sexuality reading of the issues is explicitly foregrounded. Or take the decades-long immigration ban on people with HIV migrating to the United States. This ban had an explicit sexuality bias, but it hid a concrete fear of black and brown Global South bodies. By contrast, the figure of the "welfare queen" is explicitly and racially charged, just like the immigrant family crossing a San Diego highway; yet, in both cases, their reproductive capacity and perceived deregulation make sexuality a tacit part of this equation. Take also the current Muslim travel ban working its way through the judicial system in the United States as another example of how immigration, race, and sexuality are intertwined when family relationships define who is and is not acceptable, yet this connection is not made explicit in media coverage. In these, and many other instances, the saliency of one aspect over the other calls for further exploration of the relationship between sexuality and race.

The intent behind our work in *Race and Sexuality* is to demonstrate the power relations embedded in these two axes of social reality. In this, we insist on the mutual constitution of race and sexuality as irreparably one and the same, operating in and through each other, and consider them to be two sides of the same coin. From the structural to the lived experience, the magnitude of racialized sexualities is so pertinent that political and policy analysts, as well as academics and activists, need to pay attention to them together.

In our conclusion, we address three levels of analysis that may extend the work thus far on racialized sexualities. We begin with lived experience because of its direct impact on and relevance to our everyday sensorial embodiment. We then address policy issues as institutional and mid-level indicators that have an impact but can still be shaped and negotiated through local and micro-level action. Finally, we seek to advance the academic fields of study that connect race (and class) to sexuality (and gender).

Lived experience

Racialized sexualities have a direct impact on people's everyday lives. Indeed, as stated earlier in this book, just because race and sexuality are socially constructed does not mean they can be "undone" by the individual, and it definitely does not mean these constructs do not have material, social, cultural, political, and other impacts on people's lives. As we have shown, race and sexuality are intertwined and shape people's relations to institutions, to one another, and to how they experience embodiment. In today's political and cultural climate, these experiences often unfold in neoliberal ways that put the burden of responsibility on the individual, effacing the structural and discursive ways in which people are impacted by racialized sexualities and their formations.

Even on the discursive level, figures such as the "welfare queen" or men on the "down low" shape how people in their everyday lives experience power and inequality. For example, the image of the "welfare queen" may effectively deny certain women of color access to reproductive health services or social safety nets. The stigma of HIV may discourage some people from seeking treatment at HIV clinics for fear of being seen entering the space. These processes are linked to the disparate health inequalities that people of color, especially transgender people of color, experience in society. Representations of black and Latina/o people as hypersexual or Asian people as submissive can shape intimate behaviors and experiences of online dating, where white people, who are considered the most desirable, have a range of roles in which they can embody this desire, something that is not afforded to people of color. Beauty norms and their links with race and sexuality also influence which bodies are desirable and valued and how individuals embody gender, race, sexuality, and the erotic. "Coming out" strategies – often based on white, middle-class notions of being gay – are also complicated by the ways that some people of color navigate not being heterosexual. All of these examples are part of the quotidian of racialized sexualities in the everyday world.

Likewise, the promotion of sexual rights as human rights in a global context is thought of as the prerogative of developed and progressive nations, at least superficially. But what populates this political sphere is the articulation of regulated sexual rights for women and an increasingly conservative attitude to reproductive health services and rights. Even in the most seemingly progressive countries, the regulation of gendered sexualities and reproductive rights is so ingrained that it gets restricted by the capacity for same-sex marriage and gay tourism. These are times filled with contradiction.

In the realm of sex work, race and sexuality converge in ways that shape different people's experiences of embodiment and erotic labor. With examples like cheerleaders and MILFs, white cisgender women in the sex-work market often get to engage in a variety of different embodiments. They are also more likely to do escort-type services, which is often safer than street-based prostitution. Women of color, on the other hand, are often cast in specific race-based roles, though these stereotypes can sometimes enable them to earn more in sex work and the porn industry (Miller-Young 2014; Brooks 2010). Transgender women, especially transgender women of color, also navigate sex work – often on the streets – where they are prone to harassment by the police or subject to the violence that comes with how gender, racial, and sexual norms are viewed in the public sphere.

Sexual migration is often the phrase used when people migrate for (sexuality) reasons, and this type of migration challenges notions that migratory processes are only about economic push–pull factors. People may be "sexiled" (Guzmán 1997) by family members in order to avoid other people discovering their non-heterosexual identity. Some may even migrate in order to find a sexual "freedom" that they believe exists in other countries. However, as we have noted, when people do migrate (say, to the United States), they may be able to experience being LGBT more freely but they often have to contend with racism and xenophobia. Likewise, their views on sexuality and/or their sexual identities and desires may change.

A key thread throughout this book has been how the media – as powerful social institutions – are often deeply implemented in upholding the discursive ways in which race and sexuality play out for people and suppressing other ways in which they operate. The news, entertainment, pornography, social media, and other media sources often endorse race-based sexual stereotypes about people and further these stereotypes with images that they disseminate. At the same time, the media downplay the role of sexuality in immigration, how the political is often white, heterosexual, and male. Hopefully, the "common sense" narrative that the media are implicated in relaying to the masses can be challenged through a racialized sexualities analytics.

In thinking about racialized sexualities, lived experiences are a ripe place to empirically explore these co-configurations. Through future research, the field can continue to expand, and our current understandings may be challenged, altered, and multiplied. Indeed, work is already examining how racialized sexualities affect the way that LGBT youth experiencing homelessness encounter institutions (such as the family, schools, religion) and how they navigate the streets and shelters (Robinson 2017). Work is also investigating how racialized sexualities affect mixed-race women's online dating experiences, both how the women are desired and who they desire (Buggs 2017). These new studies are just the tip of the iceberg, suggesting where racialized sexualities can lead us, or how future studies may be used to inform current research, which in turn will inform the field of racialized sexualities.

Policy making

The scholarship on racialized sexualities empowers a different kind of activism – one that may require us to connect individual narratives and experiences to contemporary social movements, and to think of these social movements as a conduit for reflecting on political aspects of our social organization, wherever we live in the world. Policy serves as one of those tools that may permit a clear engagement with, on the one hand, activist work and strategizing, and on the other, the legal and sociopolitical ways of understanding the world – which, as noted widely, is often driven by white, heteronormative assumptions about family structures and citizenry (Josephson 2016).

But, as noted in chapter 1, policy changes need to begin with the presumption that black lives matter, that women (cis and trans, and women of color in particular) deserve everyone's respect, and that while LGBT people are oppressed in the rest of the world, the Global North is itself not innocent of the violation of many people's human rights, LGBT or otherwise. When considering policy on these issues (and bearing in mind raced sexualized beings, and the regulations they face), it is also important to understand, identify, and interrogate the presumptions and unspoken rules of whiteness and heterosexuality. Given the repetitive violence that certain black and brown bodies experience, while the state focuses on "reverse discrimination" instead of addressing structural violence, policy must find a new way to explore the multitude of issues that neoliberal agendas within government structures are happy to sustain in the name of profit.

The ways in which human rights, and specifically sexual rights, are currently discussed and implemented need to be reconfigured. As we have shown, the current implementation of human rights constructs the West as progressive and the Global South as "backward," especially certain Middle Eastern and African countries. This framing ignores the ways in which sexual and gender rights are unfolding in some Global South countries that may be more "progressive" than those in the Global North. That is, the top-down, neo-imperial approach to human rights (the Global North knowing what is "best" for the Global South) upholds certain forms of domination and does not allow for the Global North learning from some Global South countries. Human rights violations within the Global North also need to be addressed, instead of the Global North merely seeing itself as the moral harbinger of other countries. The current framing of human rights only furthers a racist conceptualization of certain Global South countries, while ignoring the many gender and sexuality problems in the North. Policies and laws around transnational human rights need to change, and accountability needs to be redefined and not taken to be just what the Global North says it is – indeed, the Global North needs to be held accountable for its own human rights violations.

Debates around the criminalization and legalization of sex work have often been theoretical and abstract. As we have shown, people experience sex work differently because sex work is intimately bound up with race, class, and gender. Therefore, the decriminalization of sex work – if that is a policy goal – needs to account for the various ways in which sex work and erotic labor are experienced and shaped by racial formations. Likewise, "prostitution-free zone" laws drastically affect women of color, and especially transgender women of color, because these women are more likely to be engaged in street-based prostitution. Therefore, these types of law need to be challenged. Policy work must take care to avoid the conflation of human trafficking and other types of sex work, as not all sex work is trafficking or exploitation. Likewise, moving the framing of sex work away from disease (e.g., HIV, syphilis) could also help expand policies beyond just a public health view of the needs of sex workers.

In this current political moment, the sexualized configurations of immigration policy should be highlighted in order to better inform discussions. Indeed, notions of rape and sexual abuse have been used to justify President Trump's executive orders on immigration. The race-based sexual stereotyping of Mexicans fuels fear and hate and may not be the best basis for informed policy decisions. Likewise, the Muslim travel ban relies on sexuality – through the notion of traditional and heteronormative constructions of family – to determine who is a "good" or "safe" Muslim. Using heteronorms to inform policy is unsound. New ways of engaging the nuances of race and sexuality are needed for more inclusive immigration policies. As we have documented, though, immigration laws have always been formative of race and sexuality, and new laws and policies will potentially influence new configurations of how race and sexuality are interconnected and experienced on the meso- and micro-levels. If these laws work to expand notions of citizenship, instead of reinforcing white heterosexuality as the correct default for the "proper" citizen, then the potential for these laws to help those most marginalized may be realized.

Racialized sexualities

Race and Sexuality comes to fruition at a time when work on race and sexualities has expanded in academic organizations like the American Studies Association and the National Women's Studies Association – to name but two – and following publication of *Latina/o Sexualities* and *Black*

Sexualities (Asencio 2010; Battle and Barnes 2010), and the Race/Sex/Power Conference in Chicago in 2008 (with its tenth anniversary in 2018). This book is born around the time that the American Sociological Association's section on the Sociology of Sexualities sponsors its second pre-conference, Sexualities, Race, and Empire: Resistance in an Uncertain Time, to both think and act on aspects of such inter-articulation – in this case, engaging sociologists and social scientists in conversation and committed to moving this framework forward. At the same time, there are continuing challenges across academe, as language departments are reduced or shut down entirely in the recent trend for eliminating Latin American and other areas of study programs, mostly from the humanities. These changes in the academy are taking place within a political climate (with the current Trump administration) of impending change – with the possible dissolving of the National Endowment for the Humanities, the National Endowment for the Arts, and large cuts to the National Science Foundation budget.

These are times of pressure, and we are at a juncture where the rights that many take for granted could be erased, while conservative resistance to new rights is being fought in many places where they govern. As such, we face great challenges to produce scholarly work that surpasses the politics commonly seen in policies. Our book suggests some of the ways in which this may be accomplished, with fruitful examples that suggest further paths of research and engagement.

The work on race and sexualities continues to produce a cadre of scholars, artists, and activists who engage with the questions of our times in ways that challenge norms based on whiteness, hegemonic masculinities, and heterosexualities. This work is not just cosmetic – it activates a series of processes and suggests newer possible imaginaries of what a progressive society may be(come), without needing to call itself so.

The field of critical race studies developed without being attuned to the ways in which sexuality and gender shape and are shaped by race and racial formations, while simultaneously feminist and queer studies often lacked any analysis of race at all. There were activists' moments (e.g., the Combahee River Collective, the women-of-color reproductive rights movement, certain parts of the AIDS activist movement) that attempted to bridge these divides. Indeed, the co-constitution of race and sexuality forged the lives of these activists (e.g., access to reproductive health for women of color), and therefore addressing how these elements of race and sexuality work together had to be foregrounded in their political agendas. There were also academic interventions, most notably intersectionality, which tried to account for these gaps within the larger field of critical race, feminist, and queer studies. *Race and Sexuality* (and the field of racialized sexualities), then, is a living and ever-evolving field that sustains an analysis of certain normative assumptions outside the race/sexuality scholarship in the humanities and social sciences, and that converses with and learns from (rather than merely collecting data from) activists' and artists' contributions to this analysis.

Further research on the *structural and discursive connections* between race and sexuality should excavate previous models of theorizing race, gender, and sexuality (see, in particular, Holland 2012) that demonstrate the connections across these elements of social life. Additional research focus on the *interlocking oppressions* of race and sexualities must aim to study aspects of life beyond citizenship (Brandzel 2016) and, we would add, beyond the minoritized – that means, white heterosexual people and white gay communities should be studied not as a further universalizing of all male communities (heterosexual or gay) but precisely as indicative of norms and systems structuring everyone else's experiences. Future *methodological projects* that consider this juncture include a better connection between experimental and non-traditional research methods and race and sexuality – from autoethnographies that are not simply personal but connect to the social, to more conceptual projects of thought that count less and analyze more. (Indeed, some scholars argue for an against-queer method, given their epistemological stand or formation: see Love 2016.) More research should engage in questions of racialized sexualities in the realm of actual sexual encounters, in the ecological spaces where sexual activities take place, and, in particular, in understanding the interactions between partners in semi-public, public, and so-called private spaces.[1]

In closing

We have presented a strategy for reconsidering these two axes of social power along a continuum of disciplinary work, projects, and fields of study that are inherently interdisciplinary in nature. Our case studies insist on connecting the dots from the personal and individual to the discursive, moving through categories of nation-state and surveillance systems like immigration (asylum and refugee processes more specifically). Certainly, the focus of our case studies may present specific limitations, as would a focus based on our critical race scholarship, and feminist and queer lens – if one uses the notion of limitations to think about the work presented. We propose that to focus on something is not to constrain it. Still, although we believe other case studies would produce similar analyses, we look forward to additional published work that sustains an engagement with race and sexuality together. Our contribution is as modest as it is hopeful: modest, in that we are not the first ones to claim the need to pursue these connections and inter-articulations; and hopeful that our work will help guide learners (from all walks of life, be they professors or students, and anyone in between) into extending such analyses.

The ways in which the intimate and the everyday express and perpetuate these interlocked systems of prejudice – from racialized gendering and sexualities to sexual racism – reinforce what scholars of sexualities have been saying for a very long time: that the so-called private is political. We cast a critical gaze on the notion of individual selection and unbiased criteria, pointing out that our choices are not really menu options in à la carte neoliberal dining. We suggest that the quotidian is precisely where we should be looking first for institutional and discursive ideologies and discriminatory practices. As a research-infused and critical conversation, racialized sexualities enter a moment of uncertainty in a neoliberal, post-post-racial world, making it the more confusing to study and comprehend – that is, apprehend – but even more of an imperative for continuous engagement.

Notes

Introduction

1. When referring to race and sexuality as analytic terms, we generally retain the singular use; when referencing their co-constitutive relationship, as in racialized sexualities, we use the plural. We do this in order to (1) recognize sexuality, along with race (and ethnic) studies, as fields of study; (2) assert that there is no one form of sexuality studies, but multiple sexualities; and (3) that race and sexuality, when discussed as co-constitutive, are about the multiplicity of readings of sexuality in conversation with other axes of power – in this case, race.
2. In recent years, the emergence of a gender neutral term, Latinx, to counter the inherent gendered language in Spanish (where we say Latino for a male of Latino heritage, and Latina for a female of Latino heritage) has become popular. We generally use the Latina/o category, except when Latinx is included in a title.
3. Lesbian, gay, and bisexual are sexual orientation categories of identity; transgender is a gender identity term that only sometimes includes gender expression. Even though "sexual minorities" is a term that often encompasses gender and sexual minority groups, it is important to see how the two categories intersect: for example, transgender women (that is, women who were assigned male at birth) have a sexual orientation,

which might be heterosexual, bisexual, lesbian, pan-sexual, or something else. We note that the relationship between gender identity and sexual orientation categories has been complicated in recent work (Valentine 2007); however, it is important to also recognize that, while LGBT serves as an efficacious, coalitional term (at least in principle), gender as an institution often impacts trans women in more nuanced ways in their gendered relationship to other (mainly cisgender) women. For instance, Marcia Ochoa (2014) has documented what she coined the "accomplishment of femininity" to refer to the gendered expectations and identity-gendered labor all women engage in by looking at beauty queens and trans women who are sex workers – but is able to extend this discussion of the accomplishment to women across the board.

4. Wahneema Lubiano unpacked the racialized trope of the "welfare queen" in "Black Ladies, Welfare Queens, and State Minstrels: Ideological War by Narrative Means" (1992), an essay included in a volume edited by Toni Morrison entitled *Race-ing Justice, En-Gendering Power*. The figure of the "welfare queen" appeared in popular discourse during Reagan's administration in the early 1980s, during which the derogatory term was used to garner support for the administration's goal of reforming the USAmerican welfare system. To date, the "welfare queen" is still used to justify racialized and sexualized discrimination against (primarily) black women (Puerto Rican and other Latinas face this to a certain extent), who the trope posits as both hypersexual and irresponsible, and thus dependent on the welfare system for financial survival (see also Josephson 2016). By accusing black women of being the majoritarian recipients of welfare, of having children outside of wedlock, using welfare payments to purchase illegal substances, and engendering a racialized, poor work ethic, the imaginary of the "welfare queen" continues to shape misconceptions about public assistance.

5. We use neoliberalism to refer to discourses – based upon free market, capitalistic logics – that emphasize personal responsibility and a divestment from the welfare state and other collective political projects.

6. USAmerican references people from the United States, a country that is located in the Americas; its use takes account of non-ethnocentric geopolitics and addresses the self-centered use of

"American" by people from the United States. USAmerican better reflects the social location of people from, and living in, the United States, although there are other terms (e.g., some people use "United Staters").
7. We prefer Global North and Global South as markers of West/ rest, or first and third world countries.

Chapter 1   Two Systems Operating Synchronously

1. The session in full can be watched at the following American Sociological Association's website, and the link is provided here (accessed July 12, 2017): http://videoarchive.asanet.org/ presentation/?fw__param=protesting_police_brutality_and_ racism.
2. Smith and Frazier recently reflected on the fortieth anniversary of the Combahee River Collective Statement at Socialism 2017 conference. A video and discussion of the talk can be found here: https://shadowproof.com/2017/07/10/authors-combahee-river-statement-profoundly-influenced-black-feminism-mark-40th-anniversary/.
3. See the following *New York Times* article on the subject: https://www.nytimes.com/2015/10/06/us/publisher-promises-revisions-after-textbook-refers-to-african-slaves-as-workers. html?_r=0.

Chapter 3   Racialized Sexualization in Transnational Human Rights

1. A person engaged in sexual behavior that might be deemed (by others) as homosexual does not automatically become socially understood as a non-heterosexual person.
2. Intersex is a category of identification for people whose sex (whether defined by external genitalia or chromosomal readings) defies our binary (male/female) understanding of the sexes. Intersex is often related to lesbian, gay, bisexual, and transgender identity inasmuch as the body, gender identity, and sexual orientation are summative elements for shared activism. Intersex people are less often noted in social movements literature; thus, throughout the book, we reference LGBT, unless specified.

3. In *Voices of Internally Displaced Persons in Kenya: A Human Rights Perspective* (2015), researcher Roseanne Njiru (and co-author Bandana Purkayastha) find that, for many Kenyan women, undergoing FGS produced an increased level of sexual desirability. The complex intervention of FGS, and its understanding as FGM, exists in a contested terrain of women's rights, bodily interventions, and a challenge to cultural understandings of modernity that may be imposed onto Global South countries. Our mention is not to stake a claim in this contested terrain of being "for" or "against" FGS/FGM but, rather, to highlight how western discourses often erase the voices of women in the Global South and construct women's sexuality and bodies in/from the Global South as in a deficit against an already taken-for-granted norm.

4. The hijab refers to a head covering that covers the head, neck, and shoulders. The burka is a full-body covering which only exposes the eye area, and in some instances, exposes it only through a thin lace covering.

5. We do not want to claim that there was no discrimination against same-gender-loving people or women prior to colonization. However, colonial rules and legacy were deeply bound to codifying a great deal of discrimination in wanting to eradicate gender and sexual diversity.

6. For more on defining "two-thirds world," please see Street (2006).

7. This legacy is especially discursive in the case of Puerto Rico, which remains under a colonial power structure with the United States.

8. See: http://www.matrimonioigualitario.org/2011/07/10-razones-para-apoyar-el-matrimonio.html. Watching the video requires Spanish competency. Colombia Diversa (colombiadiversa.org) is the main LGBT watchdog organization in the country.

9. See: http://www.iglhrc.org/cgi-bin/iowa/article/pressroom/pressrelease/1417.html.

Chapter 4   Racing Sex Work

1. The different views on sex work as work or sex will be introduced later in the chapter; for now, it is important to clarify that various academics, activists, people engaged in erotic labor, policy makers, and onlookers may define sex work and

prostitution as the same or different from each other. For instance, activists who engage in prostitution with little or no recourse to condoms, infection prevention and health monitoring, and workers' benefits or formal economy workers' conditions will undoubtedly see it as anything but sex work. Although it may be unrealistic to establish this discussion as a Global North/Global South difference, suffice it to say that many Global South activists resist the sex work categorization given the dearth of humane conditions for such labor and, in that sense, the very categories (and the resources that may flow/lack from it) may produce a racialized reading (if not of colonial relations, at least of the privilege to call something by "its" name). It also goes beyond the scope of this chapter to address the sex work, abolitionist, and outlaw perspectives and debates – the strands or lines of debate and policy making that argue in favor of adjusting, reinforcing, or eliminating punishment of workers/employers.

2. Migration patterns (and their racial readings) require interrogation in general studies of migration, for sure, but also in feminist and gender studies in particular. Soderlund (2005) tracks how the effects of anti-sex trafficking language lifted pre-9/11 are now used in the United States and Europe. Similarly, Melissa Ditmore (2005) cautions us that the concerns about women's migration are intrinsically linked to ideas of mobility and economic independence, and that policies on trafficking (she discusses USAID efforts) may suggest heterosexist control of women's bodies through the economic control of international funds to one's country of origin. If it is not trafficking, but sex work, it then serves as a form of labor that produces remittances.

3. Briefly, push–pull factors refer to the reasons migrants leave their countries of origin, and the imagined or actual reasons why the countries they migrate to may offer them better opportunities. Push factors often refer to internal challenges that pressure, in some way, an otherwise seemingly voluntary migration – the self or group assessment of the "risk" of staying outweighs the potential challenges of leaving. Pull factors implicitly or explicitly reference a sense of the promise of the place sought, and while economic migration is a main reason, freedom from generally assumed conservative political or religious systems tends to also count as "pulling" them into a

certain country or region. Both push and pull factors are categorized as economic, environmental, physical, social, and cultural reasons/motivations. While migrating reasons may include a separation from families and societies of origin (including those with conservative or oppressive gendered codes of behavior and perceived gender-based oppression) and, relevant to this book, the freedom to profess a sexual behavior or identity in some ways negated in their place of origin, other more structural issues like economic reasons still tie those migrating to their families of origin (and this, too, has an impact on remittances and the establishment/sustainment of other transnational bonds). We discuss the implications of immigration to sexuality more fully in the following chapter.

4. A clear case of this script often unavailable to women of color is the "mother I'd like to f***" (MILF) imagery. Whiteness in this context is flexible and all-encompassing; in recent media coverage of the US elections, we see what some scholars call an "off-white" (Fine, Weis, Powell, and Wong 1997) East European woman, Melania Trump, who has been objectified and reduced to her erotic capital in light of her support of her husband's candidacy and election to become president of the United States of America.

5. Accessed on October 31, 2015 at http://news.bbc.co.uk/2/hi/9365967.stm.

Chapter 5   Sexualizing Immigration

1. Cantú completed his research in the 1990s, when gender and sexuality were still not accounted for as much more than just variables (for an exception, see Hondagneu-Sotelo 1994); unfortunately, Cantú died in 2002, and his work had not been published in full. His manuscript, *The Sexuality of Migration*, was published in 2009. During the time in which he conducted field research, completed his dissertation, and the book was posthumously published, an expansive body of work had been published.

2. The idea of USAmericans self-categorizing as "expats" when they voluntarily leave the United States comes to mind here. While an important topic of discussion, it falls outside the scope of this chapter. Suffice it to say, however, that only when framed within a discursive layered account of privilege may

USAmericans (or Europeans) instill the simultaneous sense of exceptionality and marginalization so ingrained in the term.

3. Migration patterns and waves are racialized and sexualized as much as they are politically different: in the migration of Cubans escaping Castro's taking over control of the country in the late 1950s, a predominantly large amount of the immigrants to the United States were light-skinned Cubans with many resources, land, and money, as well as predominantly heterosexual. In the early 1980s migration of Cubans from the Mariel port (in part, why they are called Marielitos), large numbers of the immigrants were from poor areas of the island, had been incarcerated, and were of darker skin; a significant amount of those migrating, as per Peña's contribution, were gender non-conforming sexual minorities.

4. These oppositional readings of non-whiteness and non-citizenship aligned with some non-normative sexuality and gender are also experienced by second-class citizens in the United States. Scholarship on African-American women, African-American gay men, and trans people of color attests to that – see also Brandzel (2016). Latina/o communities also experience this: in *Queer Brown Voices: Personal Narratives of Latina/o LGBT Activism* (Quesada, Gomez, and Vidal-Ortiz 2015), Letitia Gomez noted (in her oral history interview) that to be queer and immigrant in Washington, DC in the 1990s were both acts of defiance that marked those individuals as deviant and undeserving.

Conclusion: Racialized Sexualities – On Experience, Policy, and Scholarship

1. In particular, we appreciate conversations on this topic of studying actual sex in sexualities research with Angela Jones and Jason Orne. See also Orne's (2017) *Boystown: Sex and Community in Chicago*.

References

Acosta, Katie L. 2008. "Lesbianas in the Borderlands: Shifting Identities and Imagined Communities." *Gender & Society* 22(5): 639–59.

Acosta, Katie. 2013. *Amigas y amantes: Sexually Non-conforming Latinas Negotiate Family*. New Brunswick, NJ: Rutgers University Press.

Agustín, Laura M. 2007. *Sex at the Margins: Migration, Labour Markets, and the Rescue Industry*. London/New York: Zed Books.

Agyemang, Samuel. 2007. "Black Bisexually Active Men Who Do Not Disclose Sexual Activity with Men to Female Partners: An Internet Study of Factors Related to Being on the 'Down Low.'" PhD dissertation, Education, Columbia University, New York.

Ahmad, Muneer. 2002. "Homeland Insecurities: Racial Violence the Day after September 11th." *Social Text* 20(3): 101–15.

Almaguer, Tomás. 1994. *Racial Faultlines: The Historical Origins of White Supremacy in California*. Berkeley, CA: University of California Press.

Amar, Paul. 2011. "Turning the Gendered Politics of the Security State Inside Out?" *International Feminist Journal of Politics* 13(3): 299–328.

Asencio, Marysol (ed.). 2010. *Latina/o Sexualities: Probing Powers, Passions, Practices, and Policies*. New Brunswick, NJ: Rutgers University Press.

Asencio, Marysol and Acosta, Katie. 2009. "Migration, Gender Conformity, and Social Mobility among Puerto Rican Sexual Minorities." *Sexuality Research & Social Policy* 6(3): 34–43.

Ayotte, Kevin J. and Husain, Mary E. 2005. "Securing Afghan Women: Neocolonialism, Epistemic Violence, and the Rhetoric of the Veil." *Feminist Formations* 17(3): 112–33.

Barton, Bernadette. 2001. "Queer Desire in the Sex Industry." *Sexuality & Culture* 5(4): 3–27.

Battle, Juan and Barnes, Sandra L. 2010. *Black Sexualities: Probing Powers, Passions, Practices, and Policies.* New Brunswick, NJ: Rutgers University Press.

Bederman, Gail. 1995. *Manliness and Civilization: A Cultural History of Gender and Race in the United States, 1880–1917.* Chicago, IL: University of Chicago Press.

Bensonsmith, Dionne. 2005. "Jezebels, Matriarchs, and Welfare Queens: The Moynihan Report of 1965 and the Social Construction of African-American Women in Welfare Policy," in Anne L. Schneider and Helen M. Ingram (eds), *Deserving and Entitled: Social Constructions and Public Policy.* New York: SUNY Press, pp. 243–56.

Beran, Katie. 2012. "Revisiting the Prostitution Debate: United Liberal and Radical Feminism in Pursuit of Policy Reform." *Law & Inequality* 30(1).

Bernini, Lorenzo. 2015. "The Ordeal for Humanity: LGBTI Asylum Seekers in Europe Facing the Limits of Human Rights." *About Gender: International Journal of Gender Studies* 4(7): 177–89. http://www.aboutgender.unige.it, accessed December 10, 2015.

Bernstein, Elizabeth. 2007. *Temporarily Yours: Intimacy, Authenticity, and the Commerce of Sex.* Chicago, IL: University of Chicago Press.

Bernstein, Elizabeth and Schaffner, Laurie (eds). 2005. *Regulating Sex: The Politics of Intimacy and Identity.* New York: Routledge.

Berube, Allan. 2001. "How Gay Stays White and What Kind of White It Stays," in Birgit Brander Rasmussen et al. (eds), *The Making and Unmaking of Whiteness.* Durham, NC: Duke University Press, pp. 234–65.

Bonilla-Silva, Eduardo. 2013. *Racism Without Racists: Colorblind Racism and the Persistence of Racial Inequality in the United States,* 4th edn. Lanham, MD: Rowman & Littlefield.

Boykin, Keith. 2005. *Beyond the Down Low: Sex, Lies, and Denial in Black America*. New York: Carroll & Graf.

Bracke, Sarah. 2012. "From 'Saving Women' to 'Saving Gays': Rescue Narratives and Their Dis/continuities." *European Journal of Women's Studies* 19(2): 237–52.

Brandzel, Amy L. 2016. *Against Citizenship: The Violence of the Normative*. Urbana, IL: University of Illinois Press.

Brems, Eva. 1997. "Enemies or Allies? Feminism and Cultural Relativism as Dissident Voices in Human Rights Discourses." *Human Rights Quarterly* 19: 136–64.

Brents, Barbara G., Jackson, Crystal A., and Hausbeck, Kathryn. 2010. *The State of Sex: Tourism, Sex, and Sin in the New American Heartland*. New York: Routledge.

Brooks, Siobhan. 2010. "Hypersexualization and the Dark Body: Race and Inequality among Black and Latina Women in the Exotic Dance Industry." *Sexuality Research & Social Policy* 7: 70–80.

Brooks, Siobhan. 2011. *Unequal Desires: Race and Erotic Capital in the Stripping Industry*. Albany: State University of New York.

Brown, David. 2010. "Making Room for Sexual Orientation and Gender Identity in International Human Rights Law: An Introduction to the Yogyakarta Principles." *Michigan Journal of International Law* 31: 821–79.

Buggs, Shantel Gabriel. 2017. *Utopic Subjects, Post-Racial Desires: Mixed-Race, Intimacy, and the On-Line Dating Experience*. Unpublished dissertation, Department of Sociology, University of Texas–Austin.

Butcher, Kate. 2003. "Confusion between Prostitution and Sex Trafficking." *The Lancet*, June 7.

Butler, Judith. 1990. *Gender Trouble: Feminism and the Subversion of Identity*. New York: Routledge.

Butler, Judith. 2004. *Undoing Gender*. New York: Routledge.

Cahill, Sean. 2005. "Welfare Moms and the Two Grooms: The Concurrent Promotion and Restriction of Marriage in US Public Policy." *Sexualities* 8(2): 169–87.

Callis, April Scarlette. 2013. "The Black Sheep of the Pink Flock: Labels, Stigma, and Bisexual Identity." *Journal of Bisexuality* 13(1): 82–105.

Calvert, Clay and Richards, Robert D. 2006. "Porn in Their Worlds: Female Leaders in the Adult Entertainment Industry Address Free Speech, Censorship, Feminism, Culture, and the

Mainstreaming of Adult Content." *Vanderbilt Journal of Entertainment and Technology Law* 9(2): 255–99.

Canaday, Margot. 2009. *The Straight State: Sexuality and Citizenship in Twentieth-Century America*. Princeton: Princeton University Press.

Cantú, Lionel Jr. 2005. "Well-founded Fear: Political Asylum and the Boundaries of Sexual Identity in the US–Mexico Borderlands," in Eithne Luíbheid and Lionel Cantú Jr (eds), *Queer Migrations: Sexuality, US Citizenship, and Border Crossings*. Minneapolis: University of Minnesota Press, pp. 61–74.

Cantú, Lionel Jr. (with Nancy A. Naples and Salvador Vidal-Ortiz, eds) 2009. *The Sexuality of Migration: Border Crossings and Mexican Immigrant Men*. New York: New York University Press.

Carrillo, Héctor. 2004. "Sexual Migration, Cross-cultural Sexual Encounters and Sexual Health." *Sexuality Research & Social Policy* 1(3): 58–70.

Carrillo, Héctor and Fontdevila, Jorge. 2014. "Border Crossings and Shifting Sexualities Among Mexican Gay Immigrant Men: Beyond Monolithic Conceptions." *Sexualities* 17(8): 919–38.

Cervulle, Maxime. 2008. "French Homonormativity and the Commodification of the Arab Body." *Radical History Review* 100: 171–9.

Chancer, Lynn S. 1998. *Reconcilable Differences: Confronting Beauty, Pornography, and the Future of Feminism*. Berkeley, CA: University of California.

Chapkis, W. 1997. *Live Sex Acts: Women Performing Erotic Labor*. New York: Routledge.

Chauncey, George. 1994. *Gay New York: Gender, Urban Culture, and the Making of the Gay Male World 1890–1940*. New York: Basic Books.

Chavez, Leo R. 2013. *The Latino Threat: Constructing Immigrants, Citizens, and the Nation*, 2nd edn. Stanford, CA: Stanford University Press.

Cheney, Kristen. 2012. "Locating Neocolonialism, 'Tradition,' and Human Rights in Uganda's 'Gay Death Penalty.'" *African Studies Review* 55(2): 77–95.

Chin, Christine B. N. 2013. *Cosmopolitan Sex Workers: Women and Migration in a Global City*. New York: Oxford University Press.

Chin, Gabriel J. 1996. "The Civil Rights Revolution Comes to Immigration Law: A New Look at the Immigration and Nationality Act of 1965." *North Carolina Law Review* 75(1): 273–345.

Chin Phua, Voon and Caras, Allison. 2008. "Personal Brand in Online Advertisements: Comparing White and Brazilian Male Sex Workers." *Sociological Focus* 41(3): 238–55.

Chow-White, Peter A. 2006. "Race, Gender and Sex on the Net: Semantic Networks of Selling and Storytelling Sex Tourism." *Media, Culture & Society* 28(6): 883–905.

Chua, Peter and Fujino, Diana C. 1999. "Negotiating Asian-American Masculinities: Attitudes and Gender Expectations." *The Journal of Men's Studies* 7(3): 391–413.

Chun, Christine. 1996. "Mail-Order Bride Industry: The Perpetuation of Transnational Economic Inequalities and Stereotypes." *University of Pennsylvania Journal of International Business Law* 17(4): 1155.

Cohen, Cathy. 1997. "Punk, Bulldaggers, and Welfare Queens: The Radical Potential of Queer Politics?" *GLQ* 3: 437–65.

Cohen, Cathy. 1999. *The Boundaries of Blackness: AIDS and the Breakdown of Black Politics*. Chicago, IL: University of Chicago Press.

Collins, Patricia Hill. 2000 (1990). *Black Feminist Thought: Knowledge, Consciousness, and the Politics of Empowerment*, 2nd edn. New York: Routledge.

Collins, Patricia Hill. 2004. *Black Sexual Politics: African Americans, Gender, and the New Racism*. New York: Routledge.

Combahee River Collective, The. 1977. Statement. http://circuitous.org/scraps/combahee.html, accessed July 13, 2017.

Covenant Eyes. 2015. *Pornography Statistics: 2015 Edition*. Owosso, MI: Covenant Eyes.

Craig, Maxine Leeds. 2014. *Sorry I Don't Dance: Why Men Refuse to Move*. Oxford: Oxford University Press.

Crenshaw, Kimberlé. 1991. "Mapping the Margins: Intersectionality, Identity Politics, and Violence against Women of Color." *Stanford Law Review* 43(6): 1241–99.

Curington, Celeste Vaughan, Lin, Ken-Hou, and Lundquist, Jennifer. 2015. "Positioning Multiraciality in Cyberspace: Treatment of Multiracial Daters in an Online Dating Website." *American Sociological Review* 80(4): 764–88.

da Silva, Ana P. and Blanchette, Thaddeus G. 2009. "Sexual Tourism and Social Panics: Research and Intervention in Rio de Janeiro." *Souls* 11(2): 203–11.

Davis, Angela. 1981. *Women, Race, and Class.* New York: Vintage Books.

de Lauretis, Teresa. 1991. "Queer Theory: Lesbian and Gay Sexualities – An Introduction." *differences* 3(2): iii–xviii.

Decena, Carlos U. 2008. "Profiles, Compulsory Disclosure and Ethical Sexual Citizenship in the Contemporary USA." *Sexualities* 11(4): 397–413.

Decena, Carlos U. 2011. *Tacit Subjects: Belonging and Same-Sex Desire among Dominican Immigrant Men.* Durham, NC: Duke University Press.

D'Emilio, John. 1993. "Capitalism and Gay Identity," in H. Abelove, M. Barale, and D. Halperin (eds), *The Lesbian and Gay Studies Reader.* New York: Routledge, pp. 467–76.

Denike, Margaret. 2010. "Homonormative Collusions and the Subject of Rights: Reading *Terrorist Assemblages.*" *Feminist Legal Studies* 18: 85–100.

Denizet-Lewis, Benoit. 2003. "Double Lives on the Down Low." *The New York Times*, August 3.

Ditmore, Melissa. 2005. "Trafficking in Lives: How Ideology Shapes Policy," in Kamala Kempadoo (ed.), *Trafficking and Prostitution Reconsidered: New Perspectives on Migration, Sex Work, and Human Rights.* Boulder/London: Paradigm Publishers, pp. 107–26.

Doezema, Jo. 2000. "Loose Women or Lost Women? The Re-emergence of the Myth of White Slavery in Contemporary Discourses of Trafficking in Women." *Gender Issues* 18(1): 23–50.

Duggan, Lisa. 2002. "The New Homonormativity: The Sexual Politics of Neoliberalism," in Russ Castronovo and Dana D. Nelson (eds), *Materializing Democracy: Toward a Revitalized Cultural Politics.* Durham, NC: Duke University Press, pp. 175–94.

Egan, Danielle R. 2014. *Becoming Sexual: A Critical Appraisal of the Sexualization of Girls.* Cambridge: Polity Press.

Ehrenreich, Barbara and Hochschild, Arlie Russell. 2002. *Global Woman: Nannies, Maids, and Sex Workers in the New Economy.* New York: Owl Books.

Eisenstein, Hester. 2009. *Feminism Seduced: How Global Elites Use Women's Labor and Ideas to Exploit the World*. Abingdon, UK: Routledge.

El-Tayeb, Fatima. 2012. "'Gays Who Cannot Properly Be Gay': Queer Muslims in the Neoliberal European City." *European Journal of Women's Studies* 19(1): 79–95.

Epps, Brad. 2001. "Passing Lines: Immigration and the Performance of American Identity," in María Carla Sánchez and Linda Schlossberg (eds), *Passing: Identity and Interpretation in Sexuality, Race, and Religion*. New York: New York University Press, pp. 92–134.

Epstein, Steven. 1994. "A Queer Encounter: Sociology and the Study of Sexuality." *Sociological Theory* 12(2): 188–202.

Faist, Thomas, Fauser, Margit, and Reisenaner, Eveline. 2013. *Transnational Migration*. Cambridge: Polity Press.

Farrer, James and Dale, Sonja. 2014. "Sexless in Shanghai: Gendered Mobility Strategies in a Transnational Sexual Field," in Adam Isaiah Green (ed.), *Sexual Fields: Toward a Sociology of Collective Sexual Life*. Chicago: Chicago University Press, pp. 143–70.

Feliciano, Cynthia, Robnett, Belinda, and Komaie, Golnaz. 2009. "Gendered Racial Exclusion among White Internet Daters." *Social Science Research* 38: 39–54.

Ferguson, Roderick A. 2004. *Aberrations in Black: Toward a Queer of Color Critique*. Minneapolis: University of Minnesota Press.

Ferguson, Roderick A. 2012. "On the Specificities of Racial Formation: Gender and Sexuality in Historiographies of Race," in Daniel Martinez HoSang, Oneka LaBennett, and Laura Pulido (eds), *Racial Formation in the Twenty-First Century*. Berkeley, CA: University of California Press, pp. 44–56.

Findlay, Eileen J. Suárez. 1999. *Imposing Decency: The Politics of Sexuality and Race in Puerto Rico, 1870–1920*. Durham, NC: Duke University Press.

Fine, Michelle, Weis, Lois, Powell, Linda C., and Wong, Mun (eds). 1997. *Off White: Readings on Race, Power, and Society*. New York: Routledge.

Fiscella, Kevin. 2004. "Racial Disparity in Infant and Maternal Mortality: Confluence of Infection, and Microvascular Dysfunction." *Maternal and Child Health Journal* 8(2): 45–54.

Foucault, Michel. 1978 (1976). *The History of Sexuality: An Introduction*, Volume 1. New York: Vintage Books.

Frank, Katherine. 2002. *G-Strings and Sympathy: Strip Club Regulars and Male Desire*. Durham, NC: Duke University Press.

Fussell, Elizabeth, Sastry, Narayan, and VanLandingham, Mark. 2010. "Race, Socioeconomic Status, and Return Migration to New Orleans after Hurricane Katrina." *Population and Environment* 31: 20–42.

García, Lorena. 2012. *Respect Yourself, Protect Yourself: Latina Girls and Sexual Identity*. New York: New York University Press.

Garfinkel, Harold. 1967. "Passing and the Managed Achievement of Sex Status in an Intersexed Person," in *Studies in Ethnomethodology*. Cambridge: Polity Press, pp. 116–86.

González, Alfredo M. 2007. "Latinos on Da Down Low: The Limitations of Sexual Identity in Public Health." *Latino Studies* 5: 25–52.

González-López, Gloria. 2003. "De Madres a Hijas: Gendered Lessons on Virginity across Generations of Mexican Immigrant Women," in Pierrette Hondagneu-Sotelo (ed.), *Gender and US Immigration: Contemporary Trends*. Berkeley, CA: University of California Press, pp. 217–40.

González-López, Gloria. 2005. *Erotic Journeys: Mexican Immigrants and their Sex Lives*. Berkeley, CA: University of California Press.

González-López, Gloria. 2006. "Heterosexual Fronteras: Immigrant Mexicanos, Sexual Vulnerabilities, and Survival." *Sexuality Research & Social Policy* 3(3): 67–81.

Gopinath, Gayatri. 2005. *Impossible Desires: Queer Diasporas and South Asian Public Cultures*. Durham, NC: Duke University Press.

Gossett, Che. 2014. "We Will Not Rest in Peace: AIDS Activism, Black Radicalism, Queer and/or Trans Resistance," in Jin Haritaworn, Adi Kuntsman, and Silvia Posocco (eds), *Queer Necropolitics*. New York: Routledge, pp. 31–50.

Grosfoguel, Ramón. 2004. "Race and Ethnicity or Racialized Ethnicity? Identities within Global Coloniality." *Ethnicities* 4(3): 315–36.

Grzanka, Patrick R. 2014. *Intersectionality: A Foundations and Frontiers Reader*. Philadelphia, PA: Westview Press (a member of the Perseus Book Group).

Gunning, Sandra. 1996. *Race, Rape and Lynching: The Red Record of American Literature, 1890–1912*. New York/Oxford: Oxford University Press.

Guzmán, Manolo. 1997. "'Pa' La Escuelita con Mucho Cuida'o y por la Orillita': A Journey through the Contested Terrains of the Nation and Sexual Orientation," in Ramón Grosfoguel and Frances Negrón-Muntaner (eds), *Puerto Rican Jam*. Minneapolis, MN: University of Minnesota Press, pp. 209–28.

Guzmán, Manolo. 2006. *Gay Hegemony/Latino Homosexualities*. New York: Routledge.

Han, Chong-suk. 2006a. "Geisha of a Different Kind: Gay Asian Men and the Gendering of Sexual Identity." *Sexuality & Culture* 10: 3–28.

Han, Chong-suk. 2006b. "Being an Oriental, I Could Never Be Completely a Man: Gay Asian Men and the Intersection of Race, Gender, Sexuality, and Class." *Race, Gender & Class* 13(3/4): 82–97.

Han, Chong-suk. 2010. "Darker Shades of Queer: Race and Sexuality at the Margins," in Margaret L. Andersen and Patricia Hill Collins (eds), *Race, Class, and Gender: An Anthology*, 7th edn. Boston: Cengage Learning, pp. 225–61.

Han, Chong-suk. 2015. "No Brokeback for Black Men: Pathologizing Black Male (Homo)sexuality through Down Low Discourse." *Social Identities: Journal for the Study of Race, Nation and Culture* 21(3): 228–43.

Haritaworn, Jin, Tauqir, Tamsila, and Erdem, Ersa. 2008. "Gay Imperialism: Gender and Sexuality Discourse in the 'War on Terror,'" in Adi Kuntsman and Esperanza Miyake (eds), *Out of Place: Interrogating Silences in Queerness/Raciality*. York: Raw Nerve Books, pp. 71–95.

Hoang, Kimberly Kay. 2015. *Dealing in Desire: Asian Ascendancy, Western Decline, and the Hidden Currencies of Global Sex Work*. Berkeley, CA: University of California Press.

Holland, Sharon Patricia. 2012. *The Erotic Life of Racism*. Durham: Duke University Press.

Hollibaugh, Amber and Moraga, Cherríe. 2000. "What we're Rollin' around in Bed with: Sexual Silences in Feminism – A Conversation toward Ending Them," in *My Dangerous Desires: A Queer Girl Dreaming Her Way Home*. Durham, NC: Duke University Press, pp. 62–84.

Hondagneu-Sotelo, Pierrette. 1994. *Gendered Transitions: Mexican Experiences of Immigration*. Los Angeles, CA: University of California Press.

Hondagneu-Sotelo, Pierrette. 2003. *Gender and US Immigration: Contemporary Trends*. Berkeley, CA: University of California Press.

hooks, bell. 1992. "Eating the Other," in *Black Looks: Race and Representation*. Boston: South End Press, pp. 21–39.

Howe, Cymene. 2007. "Sexual Borderlands: Lesbian and Gay Migration, Human Rights, and the Metropolitan Community Church." *Sexuality Research & Social Policy* 4(2): 88–106.

Humphreys, Laud. 1970. *Tearoom Trade: Impersonal Sex in Public Places*. New York: Aldine Publishing.

Hunter, Marcus Anthony. 2010. "All the Gays Are White and All the Blacks Are Straight: Black Gay Males, Identity and Community." *Sexuality Research and Social Policy* 7(2): 81–92.

Hunter, Margaret. 2005. *Race, Gender and the Politics of Skin Tone*. New York: Routledge.

Hwahng, Sel Julian and Nuttbrock, Larry. 2007. "Sex Workers, Fem Queens, and Cross-Dressers: Differential Marginalizations and HIV Vulnerabilities among Three Ethnocultural Male-to-Female Transgender Communities in New York City." *Sexuality Research & Social Policy* 4(4): 36–59.

International Commission of Jurists. 2007. "Yogyakarta Principles: Principles on the Application of International Human Rights Law in Relation to Sexual Orientation and Gender Identity." Yogyakarta: International Commission of Jurists.

Jivraj, Suhraiya and de Jong, Anisa. 2011. "The Dutch Homo-Emancipation Policy and its Silencing Effects on Queer Muslims." *Feminist Legal Studies* 19: 143–58.

Johnson, E. Patrick. 2008. *Sweet Tea: Black Gay Men of the South*. Chapel Hill: University of North Carolina Press.

Jones, Angela. 2015. "For Black Models Scroll Down: Webcam Modeling and the Racialization of Erotic Labor." *Sexuality & Culture* 19: 776–99.

Josephson, Jyl J. 2016. *Rethinking Sexual Citizenship*. Albany, NY: State University of New York Press.

Kandaswamy, Priya. 2012. "Gendering Racial Formation," in Daniel Martinez HoSang, Oneka LaBennett, and Laura Pulido (eds), *Racial Formation in the Twenty-First Century*. Berkeley, CA: University of California Press, pp. 23–43.

Kanstroom, Daniel. 2007. *Deportation Nation: Outsiders in American History*. Cambridge, MA: Harvard University Press.

Kara, Siddharth. 2010. *Sex Trafficking: Inside the Business of Modern Slavery*. New York: Columbia University Press.

Katz, Jonathan Ned. 2005. *The Invention of Heterosexuality*. Chicago, IL: University of Chicago Press.

Katz Rothman, Barbara. 2005. *Weaving a Family: Untangling Race and Adoption*. Boston: Beacon Press.

Keck, Margaret E. and Sikkink, Kathryn. 1999. "Transnational Advocacy Networks in International and Regional Politics." *International Social Science Journal* 51(159): 89–101.

Kempadoo, Kamala. 1996. "Prostitution, Marginality and Empowerment: Caribbean Women in the Sex Trade." *Beyond Law* 5(14): 69–84.

Kempadoo, Kamala (ed.). 1999. *Sun, Sex, and Gold: Tourism and Sex Work in the Caribbean*. Lanham, MD: Rowman & Littlefield.

Kempadoo, Kamala. 2001. "Freelancers, Temporary Wives, and Beach-Boys: Researching Sex Work in the Caribbean." *Feminist Review* 67: 39–61.

Kempadoo, Kamala. 2004. *Sexing the Caribbean: Gender, Race and Sexual Labor*. New York: Routledge.

Kessler, Suzanne J. and McKenna, Wendy. 1978. *Gender: An Ethnomethodological Approach*. Chicago, IL: University of Chicago Press.

Khan, Cristina. 2015. *Reading the Body: Latina Desirability and Profit in Erotic Labor*. Unpublished MA thesis, Department of Sociology, American University.

Kibria, Nazli, Bowman, Carla, and O'Leary, Megan. 2014. *Race and Immigration*. Cambridge: Polity Press.

Kim, Joon K. and Fu, May. 2008. "International Women in South Korea's Sex Industry: A New Commodity Frontier." *Asian Survey* 48(3): 492–513.

King, J. L. 2004. *On the Down Low*. New York: Broadway Books.

Kitch, Sally L. 2009. *The Specter of Sex: Gendered Foundations of Racial Formation in the United States*. New York: SUNY Press.

Kollman, Kelly and Waites, Matthew. 2009. "The Global Politics of Lesbian, Gay, Bisexual and Transgender Human Rights: An Introduction." *Contemporary Politics* 15(1): 1–17.

Korteweg, Anna C. 2008. "The Sharia Debate in Ontario: Gender, Islam, and Representations of Muslim Women's Agency." *Gender & Society* 22(4): 434–54.

Lâm, Maivân Clech. 1994. "Feeling Foreign in Feminism." *Signs* 19(4): 865–93.

Laumann, Edward O., Gagnon, John H., Michael, Robert T., and Michaels, Stuart. 1994. *The Social Organization of Sexuality: Sexual Practices in the United States.* Chicago, IL: University of Chicago Press.

Lee, Erika. 2002. "The Chinese Exclusion Example: Race, Immigration, and American Gatekeeping, 1882–1924." *Journal of American Ethnic History* 21(3): 36–62.

Lee, Everett S. 1966. "A Theory of Migration." *Demography* 3(1): 47–57.

Leung, Rebecca. 2003. "Porn in the USA." *CBS News*, November 21.

Lewis, Hope. 1995. "Between *Irua* and 'Female Genital Mutilation': Feminist Human Rights Discourse and the Cultural Divide." *Harvard Human Rights Journal* 8: 1–55.

Lichtenstein, Bronwen. 2003. "Stigma as a Barrier to Treatment of Sexually Transmitted Infection in the American Deep South: Issues of Race, Gender and Poverty." *Social Science & Medicine* 57(12): 2435–45.

Lin, Ken-Hou and Lundquist, Jennifer. 2013. "Mate Selection in Cyberspace: The Intersection of Race, Gender, and Education." *American Journal of Sociology* 119(1): 183–215.

Llewellyn, Cheryl. 2015. *Deciding What Counts as Prosecution: An Analysis of Gender and Sexual Orientation Asylum Cases in the United States.* Dissertation, Department of Sociology, Stony Brook University.

Logan, Trevon D. 2010. "Personal Characteristics, Sexual Behaviors, and Male Sex Work: A Quantitative Approach." *American Sociological Review* 75(5): 679–704.

Lopez, Iris. 1993. "Agency and Constraint: Sterilization and Reproductive Freedom among Puerto Rican Women in New York City." *Urban Anthropology and Studies of Cultural Systems and World Economic Development* 22(3/4) (Rompiendo Barreras de Género: Social Construction of Gender in US Latino Communities): 299–323.

Lorde, Audre. 1984. *Sister Outsider: Essays and Speeches.* Trumansburg, NY: The Crossing Press.

Love, Heather. 2016. "Queer Messes." *WSQ: Women's Studies Quarterly* 44(3–4): 345–9.

Lubiano, Wahneema. 1992. "Black Ladies, Welfare Queens, and State Minstrels: Ideological War by Narrative Means," in Toni

Morrison (ed.), *Race-ing Justice, En-Gendering Power*. New York: Pantheon Books.

Lucas, Ann M. 1994. "Race, Class, Gender, and Deviancy: The Criminalization of Prostitution." *Berkeley Journal of Gender, Law & Justice* 10(1): 47–60.

Luibhéid, Eithne. 1997. "The 1965 Immigration and Nationality Act: An 'End' to Exclusion?" *positions* 5(2): 501–22.

Luibhéid, Eithne. 2002. *Entry Denied: Controlling Sexuality and the Border*. Minneapolis, MN: University of Minnesota Press.

Luibhéid, Eithne. 2004. "Heteronormativity and Immigration Scholarship: A Call for Change." *GLQ* 10(2): 227–35.

Luibhéid, Eithne. 2008a. "Queer/Migration: An Unruly Body of Scholarship." *GLQ* 14(2–3): 169–90.

Luibhéid, Eithne. 2008b. "Sexuality, Migration, and the Shifting Line Between Legal and Illegal Status." *GLQ* 14(2–3): 289–315.

Luis-Brown, David. 2008. *Waves of Decolonization: Discourses of Race and Hemispheric Citizenship in Cuba, Mexico, and the United States*. Durham, NC: Duke University Press.

Mackenzie, Sonja. 2013. *Structural Intimacies: Sexual Stories in the Black AIDS Epidemic*. New Brunswick, NJ: Rutgers University Press.

Maia, Suzana. 2012. *Transnational Desires: Brazilian Erotic Dancers in New York*. Nashville: Vanderbilt University Press.

Maira, Sunaina. 2008. "Belly Dancing: Arab-Face, Orientalist Feminism, and US Empire." *American Quarterly* 60(2): 317–45.

Manalansan IV, Martin F. 2003. *Global Divas: Filipino Gay Men in the Diaspora*. Durham, NC: Duke University Press.

Mann, Emily S., Cardona, Vanessa, and Gómez, Cynthia A. 2015. "Beyond the Discourse of Reproductive Choice: Narratives of Pregnancy Resolution among Latina/o Teenage Parents." *Culture, Health & Sexuality: An International Journal for Research, Intervention, and Care* 17(9): 1090–104.

Martinez HoSang, Daniel, LaBennett, Oneka, and Pulido, Laura (eds). 2012. *Racial Formation in the Twenty-First Century*. Berkeley, CA: University of California Press.

McClintock, Anne. 1992. "Screwing the System: Sexwork, Race, and the Law." *boundary 2* 19(2): 70–95.

McClintock, Anne. 1995. *Imperial Leather: Race, Gender, and Sexuality in the Colonial Contest*. New York: Routledge.

Mepschen, Paul, Duyvendak, Jan Willem, and Tonkens, Evelien H. 2010. "Sexual Politics, Orientalism and Multicultural Citizenship in the Netherlands." *Sociology* 44(5): 962–79.

Miller-Young, Mireille. 2010. "Putting Hypersexuality to Work: Black Women and Illicit Eroticism in Pornography." *Sexualities* 13(2): 219–35.

Miller-Young, Mireille. 2014. *A Taste for Brown Sugar: Black Women in Pornography*. Durham, NC: Duke University Press.

Minichiello, Victor, Scott, John, and Callander, Denton. 2013. "New Pleasures and Old Dangers: Reinventing Male Sex Work." *Journal of Sex Research* 50(3–4): 263–75.

Mirabal, Nancy Raquel. 2017. *Suspect Freedoms: The Racial and Sexual Politics of Cubanidad in New York, 1823–1957*. New York: New York University Press.

Mohanty, Chandra Talpade. 1988. "Under Western Eyes: Feminist Scholarship and Colonial Discourses." *Feminist Review* 30 (Autumn): 61–88.

Moraga, Cherríe and Anzaldúa, Gloria (eds). 1981. *This Bridge Called My Back: Readings by Radical Women of Color*. Watertown, MA: Persephone Press.

Morrison, Andrew R., Schiff, Maurice, and Sjöblom, Mirja (eds). 2008. *The International Migration of Women*. Washington, DC: The International Bank for Reconstruction and Development/New York: Palgrave Macmillan.

Muñoz, José Esteban. 1999. *Disidentifications: Queers of Color and the Performance of Politics*. Minneapolis: University of Minnesota Press.

Muñoz, José Esteban. 2000. "Feeling Brown: Ethnicity and Affect in Ricardo Bracho's *The Sweetest Hangover* (and other STDs)." *Theatre Journal* 52(1): 67–79.

Mutua, Makau. 2001. "Savages, Victims, and Saviors: The Metaphor of Human Rights." *Harvard International Law Journal* 42(1): 201–45.

Nagel, Joane. 2003. *Race, Ethnicity, and Sexuality: Intimate Intersections, Forbidden Frontiers*. New York: Oxford University Press.

Nakano Glenn, Evelyn. 2002. *Unequal Freedom: How Race and Gender Shaped American Citizenship and Labor*. Cambridge, MA: Harvard University Press.

Nakano Glenn, Evelyn (ed.). 2009. *Shades of Difference: Why Skin Color Matters*. Stanford: Stanford University Press.

Nash, Jennifer. 2014. *The Black Body in Ecstasy: Reading Race, Reading Pornography*. Durham, NC: Duke University Press.

Nelson, Jennifer. 2003. *Women of Color and the Reproductive Rights Movement*. New York: New York University Press.

Njiru, Roseanne and Purkayastha, Bandana. 2015. *Voices of Internally Displaced Persons in Kenya: A Human Rights Perspective*. London: Frontpage Publications.

Nobles, Melissa. 2000. *Shades of Citizenship: Race and the Census in Modern Politics*. Stanford: Stanford University Press.

Ochoa, Marcia. 2014. *Queen for a Day: Transformistas, Beauty Queens, and the Performance of Femininity in Venezuela*. Durham, NC: Duke University Press.

Ogas, Ogi and Gaddam, Sai. 2011. *A Billion Wicked Thoughts*. New York: Dutton.

Omi, Michael and Winant, Howard. 1986. *Racial Formation in the United States: From the 1960s to the 1980s*, 1st edn. New York: Routledge.

Omi, Michael and Winant, Howard. 1994. *Racial Formation in the United States: From the 1960s to the 1990s*, 2nd edn. New York: Routledge.

Omi, Michael and Winant, Howard. 2015. *Racial Formation in the United States*, 3rd edn. New York: Routledge.

Onwuachi-Willig, Angela. 2013. *According to Our Hearts: Rhinelander v. Rhinelander and the Law of the Multiracial Family*. New Haven, CT: Yale University Press.

Oppermann, Martin. 1999. "Sex Tourism." *Annals of Tourism Research* 26(2): 251–66.

Orne, Jason. 2017. *Boystown: Sex and Community in Chicago*. Chicago, IL: University of Chicago Press.

Padilla, Mark. 2007. *Caribbean Pleasure Industry: Tourism, Sexuality, and AIDS in the Dominican Republic*. Chicago, IL: University of Chicago Press.

Parker, Richard. 1999. *Beneath the Equator: Cultures of Desire, Male Homosexuality, and Emerging Gay Communities in Brazil*. New York: Routledge.

Peña, Susana. 2007. "'Obvious Gays' and the State Gaze: Cuban Gay Visibility and US Immigration Policy during the 1980 Mariel Boatlift." *Journal of the History of Sexuality* 16(3): 482–514.

Peña, Susana. 2013. *¡Oye Loca! From the Mariel Boatlift to Gay Cuban Miami.* Minneapolis, MN: University of Minnesota Press.

Pérez, Hiram. 2015. *A Taste for Brown Bodies: Gay Modernity and Cosmopolitan Desire.* New York: New York University Press.

Pessar, Patricia R. 2003. "Engendering Migration Studies: The Case of New Immigrants in the United States," in Pierrette Hondagneu-Sotelo (ed.), *Gender and US Immigration: Contemporary Trends.* Berkeley, CA: University of California Press, pp. 20–42.

Petchesky, Rosemary. 2000. "Sexual Rights: Inventing a Concept, Mapping an International Practice," in R. Parker, R. Barbosa, and P. Aggleton (eds), *Framing the Sexual Subject: The Politics of Gender, Sexuality and Power.* Berkeley, CA: University of California Press, pp. 81–103.

Peterson, M. J. 1992. "Transnational Activity, International Society and World Politics." *Millennium: Journal of International Studies* 21(3): 371–88.

Pfeffer, Carla A. 2014. "'I Don't Like Passing as a Straight Woman': Queer Negotiations of Identity and Social Group Membership." *American Journal of Sociology* 120(1): 1–44.

Phillips, Layli. 2005. "Deconstructing 'Down Low' Discourse: The Politics of Sexuality, Gender, Race, AIDS, and Anxiety." *Journal of African American Studies* 9: 3–15.

Puar, Jasbir K. 2007. *Terrorist Assemblages: Homonationalism in Queer Times.* Durham, NC: Duke University Press.

Puar, Jasbir. 2011. "Citation and Censorship: The Politics of Talking about the Sexual Politics of Israel." *Feminist Legal Studies* 19: 133–42.

Puar, Jasbir. 2013. "Rethinking Homonationalism." *International Journal of Middle East Studies* 45: 336–9.

Puar, Jasbir K. and Rai, Amit S. 2002. "Monster, Terrorist, Fag: The War on Terrorism and the Production of Docile Patriots." *Social Text* 20(3): 117–48.

Puri, Jyoti. 2012. "Sexualizing the State: Sodomy, Civil Liberties, and the Indian Penal Code," in Angana Chatterji and Lubna Chaudhry (eds), *Contesting Nation: Gendered Violence in South Asia.* Chicago, IL: University of Chicago Press, pp. 100–41.

Quan, Adam. 2002. *How to Date a White Woman: A Practical Guide for Asian Men*. Vancouver, BC: Asian World Press.

Quesada, Uriel, Gomez, Letitia, and Vidal-Ortiz, Salvador (eds). 2015. *Queer Brown Voices: Personal Narratives of Latina/o LGBT Activism*. Austin, TX: University of Texas Press.

Rahman, Momin and Jackson, Stevi. 2010. *Gender and Sexuality: Sociological Approaches*. Cambridge: Polity Press.

Reddy, Chandan. 1998. "Home, Houses, Non-Identities: Paris is Burning," in Rosemary George (ed.), *Burning Down the House: Recycling Domesticity*. Boulder, CO: Westview Press, pp. 355–79.

Reddy, Chandan. 2011. "Time for Rights? *Loving*, Gay Marriage, and the Limits of Comparative Legal Justice," in Grace Kyung-won Hong and Roderick A. Ferguson (eds), *Strange Affinities: The Gender and Sexual Politics of Comparative Racialization*. Durham, NC: Duke University Press, pp. 148–74.

Rich, Adrienne. 1980. "Compulsory Heterosexuality and Lesbian Existence." *Signs* 5(4): 631–60.

Risman, Barbara J. 1982. "The (Mis)acquisition of Gender Identity Among Transsexuals." *Qualitative Sociology* 4: 312–25.

Robinson, Brandon A. 2013. *'The Gay Facebook:' Friendship, Desirability, and HIV in the Lives of the Gay Internet Generation*. Unpublished MA thesis, Department of Sociology, University of Texas – Austin.

Robinson, Brandon A. 2015. "'Personal Preference' as the New Racism: Gay Desire and Racial Cleansing in Cyberspace." *Sociology of Race & Ethnicity* 1(2): 317–30.

Robinson, Brandon A. 2017. *Outed and Outside: The Lives of LGBTQ Youth Experiencing Homelessness*. Unpublished dissertation, Department of Sociology, University of Texas–Austin.

Robinson, Brandon A. and Vidal-Ortiz, Salvador. 2013. "Displacing the Dominant Down Low Discourse: Deviance, Same-Sex Desire, and Craigslist.org." *Deviant Behavior* 34(3): 224–41.

Ross, Marlon B. 2004. *Manning the Race: Reforming Black Men in the Jim Crow Era*. New York: New York University Press.

Ross, Marlon B. 2005. "Beyond the Closet as Raceless Paradigm," in E. Patrick Johnson and Mae G. Henderson (eds), *Black Queer Studies: A Critical Anthology*. Durham, NC: Duke University Press, pp. 161–89.

Rubin, Gayle. S. 1993 [1984]. "Thinking Sex: Notes for a Radical Theory of the Politics of Sexuality," in Henry Abelove, Michele A. Barale, and David M. Halperin (eds), *The Lesbian and Gay Studies Reader*. New York: Routledge, pp. 3–44.

Rubio-Marín, Ruth (ed.). 2006. *What Happened to the Women? Gender and Reparations for Human Rights Violations*. New York: Social Science Research Council, with support from the International Center for Transitional Justice (Canada). Advancing Transitional Justice Series.

Said, Edward. 1978. *Orientalism*. New York: Vintage.

Sassen, Saskia. 1992. "Why Migration?" *NACLA Report on the Americas* 26(2): 14–15.

Schauer, Edward J. and Wheaton, Elizabeth M. 2006. "Sex Trafficking into the United States: A Literature Review." *Criminal Justice Review* 31(2): 146–69.

Schram, Sanford F. 2005. "Putting a Black Face on Welfare: The Good and the Bad," in Anne L. Schneider and Helen M. Ingram (eds), *Deserving and Entitled: Social Constructions and Public Policy*. New York: SUNY Press, pp. 261–86.

Schulman, Sarah. 2011. "Israel and 'Pinkwashing.'" *The New York Times*, November 22.

Scott, John and Minichiello, Victor. 2014. "Introduction: Reframing Male Sex Work," in Victor Minichiello and John Scott (eds), *Male Sex Work and Society*. New York: Harrington Park Press, pp. xii–xxvii.

Sears, Claire. 2015. *Arresting Dress: Cross-dressing, Law, and Fascination in Nineteenth-Century San Francisco*. Durham, NC: Duke University Press.

Sedgwick, Eve Kosofsky. 1990. *Epistemology of the Closet*. Berkeley, CA: University of California Press.

Seymour, Craig. 2008. *All I Could Bare: My Life in the Strip Clubs of Gay Washington, DC – A Memoir*. New York: Atria Books.

Shah, Nayan. 2011. *Stranger Intimacy: Contesting Race, Sexuality, and the Law in the North American West*. Berkeley, CA: University of California Press.

Silva, Tony. 2017. "Bud-Sex: Constructing Normative Masculinity Among Rural Straight Men that Have Sex with Men." *Gender & Society* 31(1).

Skogly, Sigrun I. and Gibney, Mark. 2002. "Transnational Human Rights Obligations." *Human Rights Quarterly* 24: 781–98.

Sloan, Lacey and Wahab, Stephanie. 2000. "Feminist Voices on Sex Work: Implications for Social Work." *Affilia* 15(4): 457–79.

Smith, Amelia. 2014. "EU Court Bans Sexuality Tests for Gay Asylum Seekers." *Newsweek*, December 12.

Smith, Andrea. 2005. *Conquest: Sexual Violence and American Indian Genocide*. Cambridge: South End Press.

Soderlund, Gretchen. 2005. "Running from the Rescuers: New US Crusades against Sex Trafficking and the Rhetoric of Abolition." *NWSA Journal* 17(3): 64–87.

Somerville, Siobhan B. 2000. *Queering the Color Line: Race and the Invention of Homosexuality in American Culture*. Durham, NC: Duke University Press.

Spade, Dean. 2015 (2011). *Normal Life: Administrative Violence, Trans Politics, and the Limits of Law*, 2nd edn. Durham, NC: Duke University Press (originally South End Press).

Spivak, Gayatri. 1988. "Can the Subaltern Speak?" in Cary Nelson and Lawrence Grossberg (eds), *Marxism and the Interpretation of Culture*. Urbana: University of Illinois Press.

Steinberg, Stephen. 2007. *Race Relations: A Critique*. Stanford: Stanford University Press.

Steinbugler, Amy. 2012. *Beyond Loving: Intimate Racework in Gay, Lesbian, and Straight Interracial Relationships*. New York: Oxford University Press.

Street, Paul. 2006. "Law, Civil Society and Transnational Environmental Advocacy Networks," in Tony Shallcross and John Robinson (eds), *Global Citizenship and Environmental Justice*. Amsterdam/New York: Rodopi, pp. 95–117.

Stychin, Carl F. 2004. "Same-Sex Sexualities and the Globalization of Human Rights Discourse." *McGill Law Journal* 49: 951–68.

Surratt, Hilary L., Inciardi, James A., Kurtz, Steven P., and Kiley, Marion C. 2004. "Sex Work and Drug Use in a Subculture of Violence." *Crime & Delinquency* 50(1): 43–59.

Taormino, Tristan, Shimizu, Celine Parreñas, Penley, Constance, and Miller-Young, Mireille. 2013. *The Feminist Porn Book: The Politics of Producing Pleasure*. New York: Feminist Press at the City University of New York.

Thing, James. 2010. "Gay, Mexican and Immigrant: Intersecting Identities among Gay Men in Los Angeles." *Social Identities* 16(6): 809–31.

Thomas, Lynnell L. 2014. *Desire and Disaster in New Orleans: Tourism, Race, and Historical Memory*. Durham, NC: Duke University Press.

Thoreson, Ryan Richard. 2009. "Queering Human Rights: The Yogyakarta Principles and the Norm That Dare Not Speak Its Name." *Journal of Human Rights* 8: 323–39.

Tolnay, Stewart E. and Beck, E. M. 1990. "Black Flight: Lethal Violence and the Great Migration, 1900–1930." *Social Science History* 14(3): 347–70.

Urciuoli, Bonnie. 1996. *Exposing Prejudice: Puerto Rican Experiences of Language, Race, and Class* (Institutional Structures of Feeling Series). Boulder: Westview Press.

Valentine, David. 2007. *Imagining Transgender: An Ethnography of a Category*. Durham, NC: Duke University Press.

Valera, Pamela. 2007. "Self-Identified Heterosexual African American/Black Men Engaging in Male-to-Male Sexual Encounters: Attitudes, Behaviors and Reasons for Marriage." Columbia: School of Social Work, University of South Carolina.

Vannier, Sarah, Currie, Anna, and O'Sullivan, Lucia. 2014. "Schoolgirls and Soccer Moms: A Content Analysis of Free and 'MILF' Online Pornography." *Journal of Sex Research* 51(3): 253–64.

Vanwesenbeeck, Ine. 2001. "Another Decade of Social Scientific Work on Sex Work: A Review of Research 1990–2000." *Annual Review of Sex Research* 12: 242–89.

Vázquez-Hernández, Víctor. 2017. *Before the Wave: Puerto Ricans in Philadelphia, 1910–1945*. New York: Centro Press – The Center for Puerto Rican Studies.

Vidal-Ortiz, Salvador. 2002. "Queering Sexuality and Doing Gender: Transgender Men's Identification with Gender and Sexuality," in Patricia Gagné and Richard Tewksbury (eds), *Gendered Sexualities* (Advances in Gender Research, Vol. 6). New York: Elsevier Press, pp. 181–233.

Vidal-Ortiz, Salvador. 2009. "The Figure of the Trans-woman of Color through the Lens of 'Doing Gender.'" *Gender & Society* 23(1): 99–103.

Vidal-Ortiz, Salvador. 2014. "Keyword: 'Whiteness.'" *TSQ: Transgender Studies Quarterly* 1(1–2): 264–6.

Vidal-Ortiz, Salvador. 2016. "Sofía Vergara: On Media Representations of Latinidad," in Jason Smith and Bhoomi K. Thakore (eds), *Race and Contention in Twenty-First Century US Media*. Routledge Transformations in Race and Media Series. New York: Routledge, pp. 85–99.

Vidal-Ortiz, Salvador and Robinson, Brandon Andrew. 2016. "The Racial and Sexual Stereotypes of the 'Down Low' on Craigslist.org," in Nancy Fischer and Steven Seidmann (eds), *Introducing the New Sexuality Studies*, 3rd edn. New York: Routledge, pp. 353–62.

Vidal-Ortiz, Salvador, Viteri, María Amelia, and Serrano, Fernando. 2014. "Resignificaciones, Prácticas y Políticas Queer en América Latina: Otra Agenda de Cambio Social" ("Queer Reinterpretations, Practices, and Politics in Latin America: Another Agenda for Social Change"). *Revista Nómadas* 41: 185–201.

Waites, Matthew. 2009. "Critique of 'Sexual Orientation' and 'Gender Identity' in Human Rights Discourse: Global Queer Politics Beyond the Yogyakarta Principles." *Contemporary Politics* 15(1): 137–56.

Walker, Rebecca and Oliveira, Elsa. 2015. "Contested Spaces: Exploring the Intersections of Migration, Sex Work, and Trafficking in South Africa." *Graduate Journal of Social Science* 11(2): 129–53.

Wall, Christopher. 1998. "Human Rights and Economic Sanctions: The New Imperialism." *Fordham International Law Journal* 22(2): 577–611.

Ward, Jane. 2007. *Respectably Queer: Diversity Culture in LGBT Organizations*. Nashville, TN: Vanderbilt.

Ward, Jane. 2015. *Not Gay: Sex Between Straight White Men*. New York: New York University Press.

Weitzer, Ronald. 2009. "Sociology of Sex Work." *Annual Review of Sociology* 35: 213–43.

West, Candace and Fenstermaker, Sarah. 1995. "Doing Difference." *Gender & Society* 9(1): 8–37.

West, Candace and Zimmerman, Don H. 1987. "Doing Gender." *Gender & Society* 1(2): 125–51.

Whalen, Carmen Teresa. 2001. *From Puerto Rico to Philadelphia: Puerto Rican Workers and Postwar Economies*. Philadelphia, PA: Temple University Press.

Wilkins, Amy C. 2004. "Puerto Rican Wannabes: Sexual Spectacle and the Marking of Race, Class, and Gender Boundaries." *Gender & Society* 18(1): 103–21.

Williams, Erica Lorraine. 2011. *Sex Tourism in Bahia: Ambiguous Entanglements.* Urbana, IL: University of Illinois Press.

Wilson, Patrick A., Valera, Pamela, Ventuneac, Ana, et al. 2009. "Race-based Sexual Stereotyping and Sexual Partnering among Men Who Use the Internet to Identify Other Men for Bareback Sex." *Journal of Sex Research* 46(5): 399–413.

Wilson, Philip K. 2003. "Bad Habits and Bad Genes: Early Twentieth-Century Eugenic Attempts to Eliminate Syphilis and Associated 'Defects' from the United States." *Canadian Bulletin of Medical History* 20(1): 11–41.

Wright, Timothy. 2005. "Gay Organizations, NGOs, and the Globalization of Sexual Identity: The Case of Bolivia," in Jennifer Robertson (ed.), *Same Sex Cultures and Sexualities: An Anthropological Reader.* Malden, MA: John Wiley, pp. 279–94.

Zia, Helen. 2000. *Asian American Dreams: The Emergence of an American People.* New York: Farrar, Straus and Giroux.

Index